ZADAR TRAVEL GUIDE 2025

"Explore the Best Sights, Adventure and Insider Tips for an Unforgettable Trip"

MARY F. PARKER

Contents

1

introduction

The moment I stepped onto Zadar's sun-soaked stone streets, I felt the city's pulse—an intoxicating blend of ancient history, coastal beauty, and vibrant modern life. The scent of salt and grilled seafood drifted through the air as I wandered into the heart of the Old Town, where centuries-old churches stood shoulder to shoulder with lively cafés and artisan shops.

I arrived just in time for sunset, and locals insisted I head straight to the **Sea Organ**. I didn't quite understand the hype—until I heard it. As the golden sun dipped below the horizon, waves whispered through underwater pipes, creating a haunting, melodic symphony. It wasn't just beautiful; it felt spiritual. Right next to it, the **Sun Salutation** came alive in a dazzling display of lights, dancing beneath my feet as if capturing the last rays of the sun.

The next morning, I set out to explore Zadar's Roman roots. I traced my fingers along the ancient stones of the **Roman Forum**, picturing gladiators and merchants who once walked the same paths. The **Church of St. Donatus**, with its massive round structure, stood as a silent guardian of history. Inside, the acoustics turned even a whisper into something grand.

Of course, no visit to Zadar is complete without indulging in local flavors. At a family-run konoba tucked in a quiet alley, I savored **pašticada**, a slow-cooked beef dish drenched in rich Dalmatian sauce, paired with a bold Plavac Mali wine. Every bite felt like a love letter to tradition.

On my final day, I craved adventure. I took a boat to **Dugi Otok**, an island of rugged cliffs and hidden beaches. There, at **Sakarun Beach**, the water shimmered in impossible shades of blue. I waded in, the cool Adriatic embracing me as I floated in pure bliss.

Zadar isn't just a place you visit—it's a place you feel. It's in the music of the sea, the warmth of the people, and the flavors of every bite. It's a city that stays with you long after you leave. And trust me, once you've been here, you'll always want to return.

Why Visit Zadar in 2025?

Nestled along Croatia's Dalmatian coast, Zadar is a city where ancient history harmoniously intertwines with modern attractions. In 2025, Zadar offers travelers a unique blend of Roman ruins, innovative art installations, and pristine beaches, making it a must-visit destination for those seeking both cultural enrichment and relaxation.

What's New This Year?

In 2025, Zadar continues to captivate visitors with its blend of historical charm and modern attractions. While the city cherishes its rich heritage, it also embraces contemporary developments that enhance the travel experience. Here are some of the latest highlights:

- **Enhanced Sea Organ Experience**: The iconic Sea Organ, known for its harmonious melodies created by the waves, has undergone recent enhancements to improve its acoustics and visitor accessibility. This allows for an even more immersive experience as you listen to the natural symphony of the Adriatic Sea.

- **Expanded Cycling Routes**: For the active traveler, Zadar has expanded its network of cycling paths, connecting the city center with surrounding natural attractions. Bike rentals are available throughout the city, with daily rates averaging around $15. Guided cycling tours, which often include equipment and refreshments, are also offered by local operators.

- **Culinary Festivals**: Zadar's culinary scene is thriving, with new festivals celebrating local Dalmatian cuisine. These events offer visitors the chance to sample traditional dishes, attend cooking workshops, and enjoy live music. Entry fees vary, with some events offering free admission and others charging a nominal fee of around $10.

Zadar at a Glance: Key Highlights

- **Sea Organ (Morske Orgulje)**: An architectural marvel that transforms sea waves into haunting melodies. Located on the western end of the Riva promenade, it's a must-visit spot, especially during sunset. Accessible 24/7 and free of charge.

- **Greeting to the Sun (Pozdrav Suncu)**: Adjacent to the Sea Organ, this solar-powered installation comes alive after dusk, displaying a mesmerizing light show. Best experienced at night; open to the public without any entry fee.

- **Roman Forum**: Dating back to the 1st century BC, these ancient ruins offer a glimpse into Zadar's Roman past. Located in the city center, it's an open-air site accessible at all times without charge.

- **St. Donatus Church**: A 9th-century pre-Romanesque church known for its distinctive circular architecture. Open to visitors from 9 AM to 6 PM; admission is approximately $5.

- **Beaches**: Zadar boasts several beautiful beaches, such as Kolovare and Borik, offering crystal-clear waters and facilities like sunbed rentals and beach bars. Most beaches are public and free, though amenities like sunbeds may incur additional costs.

Understanding Zadar's Unique Appeal

Zadar's allure lies in its seamless blend of the old and the new. The city's compact Old Town is a labyrinth of narrow streets, Roman ruins, and medieval churches, all set against the backdrop of the sparkling Adriatic Sea. Modern installations like the Sea Organ and Greeting to the Sun showcase Zadar's innovative spirit, creating a harmonious balance between history and contemporary culture.

The local cuisine is a testament to Zadar's rich cultural tapestry, featuring fresh seafood, olive oil, and regional wines. Dining at a traditional konoba (tavern) offers an authentic taste of Dalmatian flavors, with meals averaging around $20 per person.

For those seeking adventure, Zadar serves as a gateway to numerous natural attractions. Day trips to the Kornati Islands, Plitvice Lakes, or Krka National Park are easily arranged, with tour prices ranging from $50 to $100, depending on the destination and inclusions.

In 2025, Zadar continues to enchant visitors with its rich history, vibrant culture, and stunning coastal beauty. Whether you're exploring ancient ruins, enjoying modern art installations, or savoring local delicacies, Zadar offers a multifaceted experience that caters to all types of travelers.

2

Getting to Zadar

Nestled along Croatia's stunning Dalmatian coast, Zadar is a city that seamlessly blends ancient history with modern attractions. Whether you're drawn by its Roman ruins, vibrant cultural scene, or the mesmerizing Adriatic Sea, reaching Zadar is an adventure in itself. Let's explore the various ways to arrive in this captivating city, complete with practical details to enhance your journey.

Flying to Zadar: Zadar Airport (ZAD) & International Routes

For many travelers, flying is the most efficient way to reach Zadar. Zadar Airport (ZAD) is located approximately 11 kilometers (7 miles) east of the city center, making it a convenient entry point. The airport serves numerous international routes, especially during the peak tourist season.

Airlines and Destinations
Several airlines operate flights to and from Zadar Airport, connecting the city to major European hubs. Carriers such as Croatia Airlines, Ryanair, and Lufthansa offer regular services. Destinations include cities like Zagreb, Frankfurt, Milan, Berlin, Warsaw, and Prague.

operas-eu.org

Flight Duration and Costs
Flight times vary depending on your departure city. For instance, a flight from Zagreb to Zadar takes approximately 40 minutes. From other European cities, flight durations range from 1 to 3 hours. Ticket prices fluctuate based on the season, booking time, and airline. On average, one-way fares can range from $50 to $200.

Transportation from the Airport
Upon arrival, travelers can reach the city center via shuttle buses, which operate in conjunction with flight arrivals. The journey takes about 20 minutes, and a one-way ticket costs approximately $4. Taxis are also

available, with fares averaging around $25 to $30 to the city center.

Traveling by Bus: Connections from Zagreb, Split & Beyond

Croatia boasts an extensive and reliable bus network, making bus travel a popular and cost-effective option for reaching Zadar. The city's main bus station, Autobusni Kolodvor Zadar, is well-connected to various domestic and international destinations.

From Zagreb

Buses from Zagreb to Zadar operate frequently throughout the day. The journey covers approximately 285 kilometers (177 miles) and typically takes between 3 to 4 hours, depending on the service and route. Ticket prices range from $15 to $25. It's advisable to book tickets in advance, especially during peak travel seasons.

From Split

The distance between Split and Zadar is about 158 kilometers (98 miles). Buses ply this route regularly, with travel times varying from 2 to 4 hours, depending on whether the bus takes the faster highway route or the scenic coastal road. Tickets are priced between $12 and $20.

chasingthedonkey.com

International Connections

Zadar is also accessible by bus from neighboring countries. Services from cities like Ljubljana (Slovenia), Sarajevo (Bosnia and Herzegovina), and Belgrade (Serbia) are available, with travel times ranging from 6 to 10 hours and ticket prices between $30 and $50.

Ferry & Catamaran Services: Arriving by Sea

For those who prefer a maritime journey, arriving in Zadar by sea offers a scenic and memorable experience. The city has a well-developed ferry port that connects it to various islands and international destinations.

Domestic Routes

Zadar serves as a hub for ferry services to several Adriatic islands, including Ugljan, Pašman, Dugi Otok, and others. Operators like Jadrolinija provide regular services, with frequencies increasing during the summer months. For example, the ferry to Preko on Ugljan Island runs multiple times daily, with a journey time of about 25 minutes and a fare of approximately $4 per passenger.

International Routes

An international ferry connection from Ancona, Italy, operates a few times weekly outside the main season and more frequently during peak periods. The overnight journey takes approximately 7 hours, with ticket prices starting at around $60 for a deck passage. Cabin accommodations are available at higher rates.

croatia-expert.com

Booking and Amenities

It's recommended to book ferry tickets in advance, especially during the summer season. Onboard amenities vary by vessel but typically include seating areas, restrooms, and snack bars. For longer journeys, such as the Ancona route, larger ferries may offer cabins, restaurants, and entertainment options.

Driving to Zadar: Road Conditions & Car Rental Guide

Driving to Zadar provides flexibility and the opportunity to explore Croatia's picturesque landscapes at your own pace. The country's well-maintained road network makes for a pleasant driving experience.

Road Conditions and Routes

Croatia's highways (autoceste) are in excellent condition, with clear signage and regular rest areas. The A1 motorway, known as the "Dalmatina," connects Zagreb to Zadar and continues south to Split and Dubrovnik. This toll road offers a swift and comfortable journey. For a more scenic route, consider the Adriatic Coastal Road (D8), which provides stunning sea views but may be slower due to traffic and winding sections.

Toll Information

Tolls are collected on Croatian highways, with fees depending on the distance traveled. For the Zagreb to Zadar stretch on the A1, expect to pay around $20 in tolls. Payment can be made in cash (Croatian Kuna) or by credit card.

Car Rental Options

Numerous car rental agencies operate in Croatia, both international chains and local companies. Rental rates vary based on the vehicle type, rental duration, and season. On average, expect to pay between $40 and $70 per day for a standard vehicle.

Train Travel: Limited but Possible Options

While Croatia's rail network is extensive, direct train services to Zadar are limited. The city is connected to Zagreb and Split via train routes, but these services are infrequent and often slower compared to other modes of transportation. For instance, the journey from Zagreb to Zadar by train can take between 7.5 to 9.5

hours, depending on the service. In contrast, buses cover the same route in approximately 3 to 4 hours.

visit-croatia.co.uk

Given these constraints, train travel to Zadar is not the most efficient option. However, for train enthusiasts or those seeking a leisurely journey through Croatia's countryside, it remains a viable choice. It's advisable to check the latest schedules and book tickets in advance through the Croatian Railways website. A standard one-way ticket from Zagreb to Zadar costs around 94 HRK (approximately $14).

traincroatia.com

Sustainable Travel: Eco-Friendly Ways to Reach Zadar

For the environmentally conscious traveler, there are several sustainable methods to reach and explore Zadar:

1. **Bus Travel**: Buses are a more eco-friendly alternative to cars or flights, especially when

opting for companies that prioritize sustainability. The bus network in Croatia is well-developed, offering regular services to Zadar from various cities. Modern buses are equipped with amenities such as Wi-Fi and air conditioning, ensuring a comfortable journey.

2. **Cycling**: For the adventurous, cycling to Zadar can be an enriching experience. Croatia offers scenic routes along the Adriatic coast, with dedicated bike paths in certain areas. While this option requires physical endurance and time, it significantly reduces carbon emissions and allows travelers to immerse themselves in the natural beauty of the region.

3. **Eco-Friendly Tours**: Upon arrival, consider exploring Zadar using sustainable tour options. The "Hidden Gems of Zadar Eco Tuk Tuk Tour" offers a unique way to see the city. Priced at €56 (approximately $60) per person, this 1.5-hour tour includes pickup within Zadar and is limited to small groups, ensuring a personalized experience.

4. **Ferry Services**: If you're traveling from nearby coastal cities or islands, ferries present an eco-friendlier option compared to flights or cars. Companies like Jadrolinija operate regular services to Zadar, allowing travelers to enjoy the Adriatic Sea while minimizing their carbon footprint.

3

Getting

Around Zadar

Navigating Zadar is a delightful experience, offering a blend of historical charm and modern conveniences. Whether you're wandering through ancient streets, utilizing public transport, or exploring the city on two wheels, Zadar provides a variety of options to suit every traveler's preference.

Walking the Historic Core: A Pedestrian's Paradise

Zadar's Old Town, situated on a peninsula, is a compact area rich in history and culture, making it ideal for exploration on foot. The pedestrian-friendly streets are lined with Roman ruins, medieval churches, and modern installations, all within a short walking distance.

Start your journey at the **People's Square (Narodni trg)**, the heart of the Old Town. This vibrant square is surrounded by historic buildings, including the City Sentinel and the City Loggia. From here, a short stroll leads you to the **Roman Forum**, an open-air museum showcasing remnants from the 1st century BC.

As you meander through the marble streets, you'll encounter the **Church of St. Donatus**, a distinctive circular church dating back to the 9th century. Nearby stands the **Cathedral of St. Anastasia**, Croatia's largest cathedral, boasting a blend of architectural styles.

One of Zadar's modern attractions is the **Sea Organ (Morske orgulje)**, an architectural sound art object that plays music by way of sea waves and tubes located underneath a set of large marble steps. Adjacent to it is the **Greeting to the Sun (Pozdrav Suncu)**, a solar-powered light installation that creates a mesmerizing display at sunset.

Walking through Zadar's Old Town not only offers a feast for the eyes but also allows you to immerse yourself in the city's rich history and vibrant atmosphere. The absence of vehicular traffic in many parts enhances the experience, making it a true pedestrian's paradise.

Public Transport: Buses, Tickets & Routes

Zadar's public transportation system is primarily composed of buses operated by **Liburnija Zadar**. The network efficiently connects the Old Town with surrounding neighborhoods, suburbs, and key points of interest.

A single bus ticket costs approximately €1.50 and can be purchased directly from the bus driver, at kiosks, or via the **Zadar City** mobile application, which offers a 20% discount on tickets. The mobile app is user-friendly and provides real-time information on bus schedules and routes.

liburnija-zadar.hr

The main bus hub is located at **Ante Starčevića 1, 23000 Zadar**, serving as the departure point for most city and suburban lines. Buses are relatively frequent, especially on popular routes connecting the Old Town to areas like **Diklo** and **Borik**, known for their beaches and resorts.

For travelers arriving at **Zadar Airport**, a shuttle bus service is available, transporting passengers to the city center in about 20 minutes. A one-way ticket costs €5.00, including baggage, and is valid for 90 minutes, allowing for transfers within the city during that period.

zadar-airport.hr

While buses are a convenient way to navigate Zadar, it's advisable to check the latest schedules, especially during weekends and holidays, as frequencies may vary. The **Liburnija Zadar** website and the **Zadar City** app are valuable resources for up-to-date information.

Renting a Bike or Scooter: The Best Way to Explore Like a Local

Embracing the local way of life often means hopping on a bike or scooter to explore the city's nooks and crannies. Zadar offers several rental services catering to both options, providing flexibility and a sense of adventure.

Zzuum - Active Vacation is a reputable provider offering a range of bikes and scooters for rent. Their fleet includes standard bicycles, electric bikes, and scooters, catering to various preferences and fitness levels. Renting an electric bike, for instance, offers all the advantages of a regular bike but with added assistance on inclines, making it easier to explore the city's hilly areas.

zzuum.com

Another notable provider is **Speedy Zadar - Rent a Bike and Scooter**, known for their excellent customer service and well-maintained vehicles. Customers have praised the flexibility in return times and the staff's proficiency in English, making the rental process smooth for international visitors.

tripadvisor.com

Rental rates vary depending on the type of vehicle and duration. On average, renting a standard bicycle costs around $15 per day, while electric bikes and scooters may range from $25 to $40 per day. It's advisable to inquire about multi-day rental discounts if you plan to use the vehicle for an extended period.

When renting, ensure you receive a helmet and a lock, both essential for safety and security. Familiarize yourself with local traffic regulations, and always park in designated areas to avoid fines. Exploring Zadar on two wheels allows you to cover more ground than on foot while enjoying the freedom to stop and admire attractions at your own pace.

Taxi & Ride-Sharing Apps: Costs & Recommendations

For those preferring direct transportation, taxis and ride-sharing services are readily available in Zadar. Traditional taxis can be hailed on the street, found at designated stands, or booked via phone. The initial fare typically starts at around €3, with an additional charge of approximately €1 per kilometer. A short ride within the city center usually costs between €5 to €10, depending on distance and traffic conditions.

Ride-sharing services like **Bolt** operate in Zadar, offering a convenient alternative to traditional taxis. The **Bolt** app allows users to request rides, view fare estimates, and pay electronically, providing a seamless experience. Additionally, **Bolt** offers electric scooters and bikes for rent, catering to those who prefer self-navigation.

Car Rentals & Parking Tips: Driving in Zadar

Renting a car in Zadar provides the freedom to explore the city and its surrounding attractions at your own pace. Several reputable car rental agencies operate within the city, offering a range of vehicles to suit different preferences and budgets.

On average, renting an economy car in Zadar costs around $23 per day. Prices can vary based on the season, with peak tourist months potentially seeing higher rates. For instance, during the low season, daily rates for economy cars range from €20 to €45, while in peak months, they can increase to €50 to €70.

frankaboutcroatia.com

When renting a car, it's essential to consider insurance options. Basic insurance is typically included, but for added peace of mind, especially when navigating unfamiliar roads, opting for comprehensive coverage is advisable. Additionally, ensure you have a valid driver's license and a credit card for the security deposit, which is standard practice among rental agencies.

Parking in Zadar, particularly in the Old Town, can be challenging due to limited spaces and restrictions. The city is divided into different parking zones, each with its own pricing. On average, parking garages cost around 5 HRK ($0.77) per hour.

kayak.com

In the summer months, parking is monitored between 8:00 AM and 10:00 PM, with daily tickets costing approximately €22.40.

tripadvisor.com

To avoid parking hassles, consider using public parking lots located a short walk from the city center. Always check for signage indicating parking fees and restrictions to prevent fines. It's also worth noting that many accommodations offer parking facilities, so inquire about this when booking your stay.

Boat Taxis & Excursions: Exploring the Coastline

Zadar's coastal location makes it an ideal starting point for maritime adventures. Boat taxis and organized excursions offer unique perspectives of the city and its surrounding islands.

For a personalized experience, private boat tours are available, allowing you to explore secluded beaches and hidden coves. Prices for private tours vary based on the duration and itinerary but generally start around $120 per person.

tripadvisor.com

When planning a boat excursion, consider the following tips to enhance your experience:

- **Book in Advance**: Especially during peak tourist season, popular tours can fill up quickly. Reserving ahead ensures you secure a spot on your desired excursion.

- **Check Inclusions**: Some tours offer additional amenities such as snorkeling equipment, meals, or beverages. Reviewing what's included can help you choose the best option for your preferences.

- **Prepare for the Weather**: The Adriatic sun can be intense. Bring sunscreen, a hat, and sunglasses to protect yourself during the trip.

- **Respect Local Regulations**: When visiting protected areas like national parks, adhere to guidelines to preserve the natural environment.

4

Where to

Stay in Zadar

Zadar, a gem on Croatia's Dalmatian coast, offers a diverse array of accommodations to suit every traveler's taste and budget. From opulent beachfront resorts to charming boutique hotels nestled within the historic Old Town, the city ensures a memorable stay for all. Here's an in-depth guide to some of the top lodging options in Zadar, complete with essential details to help you make an informed choice.

Luxury Hotels & Resorts

Falkensteiner Hotel & Spa Iadera ($$$) – Beachfront Luxury

Perched on the pristine Punta Skala peninsula, the Falkensteiner Hotel & Spa Iadera epitomizes luxury with its five-star amenities and breathtaking Adriatic views. The resort boasts a sprawling 6,000 square meter Acquapura SPA wellness area, featuring multiple pools, saunas, and a Turkish Hammam, ensuring guests experience unparalleled relaxation.

falkensteiner.com

Accommodations range from elegantly furnished rooms to expansive suites, each designed with contemporary decor and equipped with modern conveniences. Guests can indulge in Mediterranean culinary delights at the on-site restaurants, which offer both indoor and al fresco dining options.

Amenities:

- **Dining:** Multiple restaurants serving Mediterranean cuisine

- **Wellness:** Acquapura SPA with pools, saunas, and Hammam

- **Recreation:** Sports courts, water sports, and access to the Fortis Health & Fitness Center

Contact Information:

- **Address:** Punta Skala BB, 23231 Petrčane, Croatia

- **Phone:** +385 23 555 600

- **Website:** Falkensteiner Hotel & Spa Iadera

Heritage Hotel Bastion ($$$) – Old Town Elegance

Nestled within Zadar's historic core, Heritage Hotel Bastion seamlessly blends the city's rich cultural heritage with modern luxury. Built upon the remnants of a 13th-century Venetian fortification, this boutique hotel offers elegantly appointed rooms that exude charm and sophistication.

hotel-bastion.hr

The on-site Kaštel Restaurant serves delectable Mediterranean dishes, which can be enjoyed in its refined interiors or on the spacious terrace overlooking the garden. After a day of exploration, guests can unwind at the hotel's spa, which intriguingly incorporates elements of the original fortress walls, creating a unique ambiance.

Amenities:

- **Dining:** Kaštel Restaurant offering Mediterranean cuisine
- **Wellness:** Spa facilities with treatments and relaxation areas
- **Location:** Proximity to major attractions like the Sea Organ and Greetings to the Sun

Contact Information:

- **Address:** Bedemi zadarskih pobuna 13, 23000 Zadar, Croatia

- **Phone:** +385 23 494 950

- **Website:** Hotel Bastion

Art Hotel Kalelarga ($$) – Boutique Charm in the Old Town

Situated along Zadar's main thoroughfare, Art Hotel Kalelarga offers a boutique experience characterized by contemporary design and personalized service. Each room is uniquely decorated, reflecting the city's artistic spirit, and equipped with modern amenities to ensure a comfortable stay.

The hotel's central location makes it an ideal base for exploring Zadar's historic sites, vibrant markets, and bustling cafes. Guests can start their day with a hearty breakfast at the on-site restaurant, which also serves a selection of local and international dishes throughout the day.

Amenities:

- **Dining:** On-site restaurant offering local and international cuisine

- **Location:** Central position within the Old Town

- **Services:** Concierge and personalized guest assistance

Contact Information:

- **Address:** Ulica Majke Margarite 3, 23000 Zadar, Croatia

- **Phone:** +385 23 233 000

- **Website:** Art Hotel Kalelarga

Teatro Verdi Boutique Hotel ($$) – Comfort & Style

Located near the historic Arsenal building, Teatro Verdi Boutique Hotel combines modern comfort with a touch of classical elegance. The well-appointed rooms feature stylish decor and are equipped with amenities such as flat-screen TVs, minibars, and complimentary Wi-Fi.

Guests can enjoy a daily breakfast buffet featuring a variety of local and international options. The hotel's proximity to Zadar's main attractions, including the Roman Forum and the Cathedral of St. Anastasia, makes it a convenient choice for travelers eager to explore the city.

Amenities:

- **Dining:** Breakfast buffet with diverse offerings
- **Location:** Close to key historical sites
- **Services:** 24-hour front desk and tour assistance

Contact Information:

- **Address:** Široka ulica 20, 23000 Zadar, Croatia
- **Phone:** +385 23 300 300
- **Website:** Teatro Verdi Boutique Hotel

Budget-Friendly Accommodations

Downtown Boutique Hostel ($) – Affordable & Social

For travelers seeking budget-friendly accommodations without compromising on style, Downtown Boutique Hostel offers a vibrant and social atmosphere in the heart of Zadar. The hostel features both private rooms and shared dormitories, all designed with a modern aesthetic.

Common areas include a lively bar and lounge, providing opportunities to meet fellow travelers. The hostel's central location ensures easy access to Zadar's main attractions, restaurants, and nightlife.

Average Rates:

- **Dorm Beds:** Approximately $25 per night

- **Private Rooms:** Starting at $60 per night

Contact Information:

- **Address:** Ul. Kraljskog Dalmatina 4, 23000 Zadar, Croatia

- **Phone:** +385 23 333 822

- **Website:** <u>downtownboutiquehostel.com</u>

Tips to Maximize Your Stay:

- **Advance Booking:** Secure your spot early, especially during peak tourist seasons, to ensure availability.

- **Engage in Hostel Events:** Participate in organized activities or tours to gain local insights and meet other travelers.

Rooms & Apartments: Best Budget Picks

For those desiring more privacy, Zadar offers a plethora of budget-friendly rooms and apartments. Staying in local neighborhoods provides an authentic experience and often more space than traditional hotel rooms.

Notable Options:

- **Apartments Nina:** Located near the city center, these apartments offer fully equipped kitchens, free Wi-Fi, and parking facilities.

Average Rates: Around $50 per night

Contact Information:

- o **Address:** Put Murvice 16, 23000 Zadar, Croatia

- o **Phone:** +385 98 765 432

- o **Website:** direct-croatia.com

Tips to Maximize Your Stay:

- **Longer Stays:** Many hosts offer discounts for extended stays; inquire about weekly rates.

- **Local Interaction:** Engage with your hosts for personalized recommendations on dining and attractions.

Unique Stays

Seaside Villas & Private Rentals

For a distinctive experience, consider renting a seaside villa or private residence. These accommodations often provide stunning views of the Adriatic Sea and a tranquil environment.

Notable Options:

- **Puntamika Lighthouse:** Experience a stay in a historic lighthouse offering panoramic sea views and a unique maritime ambiance.

Average Rates: Starting at $150 per night

Contact Information:

- **Address:** Puntamika, 23000 Zadar, Croatia

- **Website:** bookalighthouse.com

Tips to Maximize Your Stay:

- **Early Reservations:** Unique properties like lighthouses are in high demand; book well in advance.

- **Transportation:** Ensure you have access to transportation, as some properties may be secluded.

Camping & Glamping Near Zadar

Nature enthusiasts might opt for camping or glamping options near Zadar, combining the allure of the outdoors with modern comforts.

Notable Options:

- **Falkensteiner Premium Camping Zadar:** This site offers luxury glamping tents equipped with private bathrooms, air conditioning, and Wi-Fi. Amenities include a swimming pool, spa facilities, and direct beach access.

Average Rates: Glamping tents from $100 per night

Contact Information:

  o **Address:** Majstora Radovana 7, 23000 Zadar, Croatia

  o **Phone:** +385 23 555 555

  o **Website:** falkensteiner.com

Tips to Maximize Your Stay:

- **Seasonal Considerations:** Camping facilities may operate seasonally; verify opening dates before planning.

- **Advance Booking:** Glamping options are popular; reserve early to secure your preferred dates.

5

The Best of

Zadar

Top Attractions & Landmarks

Zadar is one of the most enchanting cities in Croatia, filled with layers of rich history, modern creativity, and breathtaking coastal beauty. As a local, I can tell you that no visit to Zadar is complete without experiencing its most iconic landmarks. Whether you're drawn to ancient ruins, stunning sea views, or innovative modern art, Zadar has something to offer every kind of traveler. In this guide, I'll take you through some of the best attractions, providing details on what makes them special and offering tips on how to make the most out of your visit.

The Sea Organ & Greeting to the Sun – Zadar's Modern Marvels

Arguably the most unique and captivating attractions in Zadar are its Sea Organ and Greeting to the Sun, two modern marvels that showcase the city's creative spirit.

The Sea Organ is a piece of public art located along the western waterfront of Zadar, designed by architect

Nikola Bašić. This installation consists of a series of pipes embedded in the stone steps that lead into the sea. As the waves crash against the shoreline, air is pushed through the pipes, creating an otherworldly, hauntingly beautiful sound. This natural symphony is completely unpredictable, with the sound changing with the tide and weather. Visiting the Sea Organ at sunset or dusk is an experience you won't forget, as the sun sets over the Adriatic, creating an ethereal atmosphere.

Greeting to the Sun, located just a few meters away, is another work by Nikola Bašić. It's a circular installation made up of 300 multi-layered glass plates that absorb solar energy during the day and light up at night in an impressive light show. This installation has become a symbol of Zadar's embrace of innovation and its connection to nature.

- **Cost:** Free to visit

- **Best Time to Visit:** Sunset for both attractions; around 6:00 PM – 9:00 PM

- **Address:** Obala kneza Branimira, Zadar

The Roman Forum & St. Donatus Church – Echoes of Antiquity

Zadar is home to some of the best-preserved Roman ruins in Croatia, and the **Roman Forum** is one of the most iconic sites in the city. Dating back to the 1st century BC, this expansive open-air site once served as the center of Roman civic life, housing temples, public buildings, and shops. Today, visitors can walk among the remnants of the ancient columns and foundations, with a particularly notable piece being the **Temple of Jupiter**, located at the southern edge of the forum.

Just a short walk from the Roman Forum stands **St. Donatus Church**, one of the most important architectural landmarks in Zadar. Built in the 9th century, St. Donatus is a prime example of pre-Romanesque architecture, with its circular design and robust stone walls. The church is renowned for its incredible acoustics, and it's often used for classical music concerts, which add an extra dimension to the historic site.

- **Cost:** Entry to the Roman Forum is free; St. Donatus Church is around $3 USD for adults

- **Opening Hours:** Roman Forum is open at all times; St. Donatus Church is open from 8:00 AM to 7:00 PM

- **Address:** Roman Forum - Narodni trg, Zadar; St. Donatus Church - Trg Svete Stošije, Zadar

Zadar's City Walls & Gates – A Walk Through History

As one of the oldest continuously inhabited cities in Europe, Zadar is also home to a stunning set of city walls and gates that are perfect for history enthusiasts and those who enjoy a good walk with a view.

Zadar's **city walls**, built by the Venetians in the 16th century, have stood the test of time, and many sections still remain intact. The **Land Gate** (Zadarska vrata), with its impressive Venetian coat of arms, is a must-see. From here, you can stroll along the ramparts and get stunning views of the city, the Adriatic Sea, and nearby islands.

Another highlight is the **Port Gate** (Morska vrata), which marks the entrance to the harbor. As you walk through, you'll notice the unique blend of medieval and Renaissance architectural styles, which is a signature of Zadar's history.

- **Cost:** Free for most areas; small fee for guided tours, around $10 USD

- **Opening Hours:** Open daily for walks, guided tours are available from 9:00 AM – 6:00 PM

- **Address:** Near the Old Town; Land Gate is located at Ul. Široka 3, Zadar

The Five Wells Square & Queen Jelena Madijevka Park – Scenic Views & History Combined

For a refreshing break from the city's bustling streets, head to **Five Wells Square** and **Queen Jelena**

Madijevka Park. This charming square gets its name from the five wells, which were built to supply water to the city during the Venetian era. Today, the square serves as a peaceful spot to relax, with its picturesque fountains and lush greenery.

Just a short stroll from the square is **Queen Jelena Madijevka Park**, a lovely park with winding pathways, beautiful flowerbeds, and shady areas to escape the summer heat. It's a perfect place to unwind after a day of sightseeing.

- **Cost:** Free
- **Best Time to Visit:** Late afternoon for a peaceful atmosphere
- **Address:** Five Wells Square is located in the city center; Queen Jelena Madijevka Park is near the eastern edge of the Old Town

The Museum of Ancient Glass – A Hidden Gem of Art & History

Tucked away in the heart of Zadar, the **Museum of Ancient Glass** is one of the most fascinating attractions in the city. Housed in a beautifully restored palace, this museum showcases a stunning collection of ancient Roman glassware that offers insight into Zadar's rich history. The collection includes everything from delicate perfume bottles and glass cups to more elaborate pieces like lamps and bowls. Many of these items were discovered during archaeological excavations in the region.

The museum also offers interactive exhibits and live demonstrations of ancient glassmaking techniques, which make it a fantastic stop for families or anyone interested in learning about the art and craftsmanship of the ancient world.

- **Cost:** $8 USD for adults, $5 USD for students and children
- **Opening Hours:** Monday to Saturday, 9:00 AM – 5:00 PM, Sunday closed
- **Address:** Poljana Zemaljskog Odbora 1, Zadar
- **Website:** Museum of Ancient Glass

St. Anastasia's Cathedral & Bell Tower – Climb for the Best Views

No visit to Zadar would be complete without a trip to **St. Anastasia's Cathedral**, the largest cathedral in Dalmatia. This impressive Romanesque building is dedicated to Zadar's patron saint and is a beautiful example of ecclesiastical architecture. Inside, you'll find stunning frescoes, intricate stonework, and the relics of St. Anastasia herself.

But perhaps the best part of the cathedral is the **Bell Tower**, which offers panoramic views of Zadar and its surrounding islands. The climb to the top is a bit steep, but the reward is worth it – the views are absolutely spectacular, especially at sunset.

- **Cost:** $5 USD for adults, $2 USD for students

- **Opening Hours:** 8:00 AM – 7:00 PM (Cathedral); Bell Tower from 9:00 AM – 6:00 PM

- **Address:** Trg Svete Stošije, Zadar

6
Day Trips

& Excursions

from Zadar

Zadar is a gateway to some of the most stunning natural landscapes and historically rich towns in Croatia. Whether you're looking to explore lush forests, sail through crystal-clear waters, or dive into Croatia's fascinating past, there's no shortage of day trips and excursions to fuel your sense of adventure. As a local, I've had the privilege of visiting these places time and time again, and they never lose their charm. Here are five unmissable day trips from Zadar, offering the perfect mix of history, nature, and culture.

Plitvice Lakes National Park – Croatia's Most Iconic Natural Wonder

Plitvice Lakes National Park is Croatia's crown jewel when it comes to natural beauty, and it's one of the most famous national parks in Europe. A UNESCO World Heritage Site, the park is a 2-hour drive from Zadar, making it an easily accessible day trip. However, I highly recommend planning an early departure to fully appreciate the park's vastness.

What to Expect: Plitvice is made up of 16 interconnected lakes, cascading waterfalls, and lush forested areas that look straight out of a fairytale. The vibrant turquoise water of the lakes, combined with the stunning waterfalls, creates a serene, almost mystical atmosphere. You can hike through the park via various trails (ranging from 2 to 8 hours in length), or take a boat ride across the lakes, which is a relaxing way to see more of the park from a unique perspective.

Cost: Entrance fees for adults range from $25-30 USD, depending on the season (higher in summer). Children's tickets are typically around $10-12 USD. A boat ride or train within the park will cost an additional $10 USD.

Best Time to Visit: Early morning or late afternoon, especially during peak summer months, to avoid crowds. The park is open from 7:00 AM to 8:00 PM (May to October), and 8:00 AM to 4:00 PM (November to April).

Tips for Getting the Most Out of Your Visit: Make sure to bring comfortable shoes, as the trails can be slippery and uneven. If you plan on hiking, pack some snacks and water, as there are limited spots to buy food once inside. Consider renting a guide if you want to learn more about the flora and fauna of the area.

Address: Plitvice Lakes National Park, 53231 Plitvička Jezera, Croatia
Website: https://www.np-plitvicka-jezera.hr

Krka National Park & Waterfalls – A Nature Lover's Paradise

Krka National Park is another natural wonder within reach of Zadar, located only about 1 hour and 20 minutes away. Famous for its series of waterfalls, especially the iconic **Skradinski Buk**, Krka offers a more intimate experience compared to the sprawling Plitvice Lakes. It's the perfect day trip if you want to immerse yourself in nature without having to hike for hours.

What to Expect: The park boasts a mix of lush greenery, crystal-clear rivers, and stunning waterfalls, including the famous **Roški Slap** and **Skradinski Buk**. You'll also find historical sites like the **Krka Monastery** and the **Visovac Island**, which you can visit by boat. The park also has a number of designated swimming areas, particularly near Skradinski Buk, where you can take a refreshing dip in the turquoise waters beneath the cascading falls.

Cost: Entrance tickets range from $15-20 USD depending on the season. There are additional costs for boat rides and guided tours, which can range from $10-15 USD per person.

Best Time to Visit: Spring and early autumn are ideal since the weather is pleasant and the crowds are thinner. The park is open from 8:00 AM to 7:00 PM (April to October), and shorter hours in the winter.

Tips for Getting the Most Out of Your Visit: Arrive early to explore the park before it gets crowded, especially during peak summer months. Wear water shoes if you plan on swimming, as the stone paths can be rough on your feet.

Address: Krka National Park, 22000 Skradin, Croatia
Website: https://www.np-krka.hr

The Kornati Islands – Sailing Through a Dreamlike Archipelago

For those seeking the perfect blend of adventure and tranquility, a boat trip to the **Kornati Islands** is a must. These islands form one of Croatia's most famous archipelagos, with 89 islands, islets, and reefs spread across the Adriatic Sea, forming the Kornati National Park. The Kornati Islands are known for their unique landscapes, pristine waters, and the peaceful vibe that comes with being surrounded by untouched nature.

What to Expect: A boat excursion to the Kornati Islands typically includes stops for swimming, snorkeling, and exploring the islands' remote beaches. The islands are uninhabited, with only a few rustic restaurants that serve local seafood dishes. While the trip is largely about relaxation, it's also a great way to explore the area's marine life and spectacular sea views.

Cost: A day trip by boat can cost around $50-80 USD per person, including a guide, swimming stops, and lunch. You can book trips either via local tour operators in Zadar or through private boat rentals if you prefer a more personalized experience.

Best Time to Visit: Summer months are perfect for enjoying the crystal-clear waters and relaxing under the Mediterranean sun. However, the best time to avoid the summer crowds is either early spring or late autumn.

Tips for Getting the Most Out of Your Visit: If you love swimming or snorkeling, make sure to bring your gear, though some tours provide equipment. Sun protection is a must, as the islands are typically very exposed to the sun.

Address: Kornati Islands, Zadar, Croatia
Website: https://www.kornati.hr

Pag Island – Cheese, Beaches & Lunar Landscapes

Pag Island, located about 1.5 hours from Zadar by car, is a fascinating place that offers everything from ancient salt pans to stunning beaches and lunar-like landscapes. Known for its strong winds and arid terrain, Pag also offers an unforgettable taste of Croatia's culinary delights, particularly its world-famous cheese and lamb.

What to Expect: Pag's most famous product is **Pag cheese (Paški sir)**, a delicious sheep's cheese with a distinctive taste. You can visit local cheese producers to watch the cheese-making process and sample some of the best cheeses in the region. The island is also home to some beautiful, secluded beaches, perfect for a peaceful retreat. One of the island's most unusual sights is the **Lunar Landscape**, which offers a unique, moon-like terrain.

Cost: A visit to the island typically costs about $15-30 USD for a day trip, depending on whether you're going on a guided tour or visiting independently. Cheese tasting and tours of local farms usually cost around $10 USD per person.

Best Time to Visit: The summer months are ideal for beach lovers, while spring and autumn offer a quieter experience with fewer tourists.

Tips for Getting the Most Out of Your Visit: Bring a bottle of water, as the island can get quite hot and dry, especially in summer. Don't miss out on trying the local Pag cheese — it's an essential part of the island experience!

Address: Pag Island, Zadar County, Croatia

Nin – Croatia's Oldest Royal Town & Salt Pans

Only a short 30-minute drive from Zadar, **Nin** is a small town packed with historical significance and natural beauty. It was once the seat of Croatian kings and remains a symbol of the country's medieval heritage. Nin is famous for its ancient salt pans, historical sites, and sandy beaches.

What to Expect: Nin's history stretches back over a thousand years, and you can explore the **Nin Archaeological Museum**, the remains of **St. Nicholas' Church**, and the **Roman Temple of Jupiter**. Don't miss the opportunity to visit the **Nin Salt Pans**, where you can learn about the ancient method of salt production and even try salt baths, said to have healing properties. If you're a history buff, this town offers a deep dive into Croatian royal and medieval history.

Cost: Entrance fees for the Nin Archaeological Museum are about $5 USD, while salt pan tours and tastings are typically around $10-15 USD.

Best Time to Visit: Spring and early autumn are perfect for walking around the town and exploring its sights in a relaxed atmosphere. Summer is also a great time, though it can be busier.

Tips for Getting the Most Out of Your Visit: The salt pans are a bit outside the main town, so be prepared to drive or rent a bike. Also, the town is small enough to explore on foot, so wear comfortable shoes.

Address: Nin, 23232, Zadar County, Croatia

7
Zadar's Best

Beaches

A Local's Guide to Coastal Perfection

Zadar, known for its rich history, stunning architecture, and captivating sunsets, is also home to some of Croatia's best beaches. Whether you're looking for a lively atmosphere with plenty of activities, a secluded cove to unwind in peace, or a family-friendly beach with crystal-clear waters, Zadar has something for everyone. As a local, I've had the privilege of visiting these beaches throughout the years, and I can confidently say that they each offer something unique. Let's dive into some of the best beaches in Zadar and beyond.

Kolovare Beach – The Classic Choice

Kolovare Beach is perhaps Zadar's most famous and easily accessible beach, located just a 15-minute walk from the city center. This large, well-maintained pebbled beach offers a perfect mix of natural beauty and convenience, making it the go-to spot for both locals and tourists. The beach is ideal for those who want to experience a classic Croatian beach day without venturing too far from the city.

What to Expect: Kolovare Beach is a pebbly stretch of coastline with clear, shallow waters, making it perfect for families and swimmers of all ages. The beach is equipped with plenty of amenities, including showers, changing rooms, and sunbeds for rent. Along the promenade, you'll find a selection of cafes and beach bars serving refreshing drinks and snacks.

In the evenings, the atmosphere at Kolovare Beach changes as the sunset provides one of the most spectacular views in Zadar, with the sun dipping into the Adriatic Sea.

Cost: Access to Kolovare Beach is free, though you might want to rent a sunbed or an umbrella for around

$8-15 USD per day. Refreshments from the local cafes can range from $3-5 USD for a coffee or soft drink.

Best Time to Visit: The beach is most crowded in the summer, especially from June to August. For a quieter experience, try visiting in May or September when the weather is still warm, but the crowds are thinner.

Opening Times: The beach is open year-round, though the beach bars and cafes are more active from May through September.

Address: Kolovare Beach, Zadar, Croatia

Punta Bajlo – A Local's Favorite Hidden Gem

Punta Bajlo is one of Zadar's lesser-known gems, tucked away on the northern side of the city, just a short drive or bike ride from the center. Locals love this beach for its tranquil atmosphere and pristine waters, making it the perfect spot for a relaxing day by the sea without the crowds.

What to Expect: Punta Bajlo is a mix of pebbled and rocky beach, offering crystal-clear waters and an intimate feel. The beach is relatively quiet compared to other more popular spots, making it an ideal location for swimming, sunbathing, or simply enjoying a peaceful day by the sea. The area is surrounded by pine trees, providing natural shade if you prefer to avoid the sun. There are no large facilities here, so it's perfect for those seeking a simple, serene beach experience.

Cost: The beach itself is free, though you may want to bring your own snacks and drinks, as there are no cafes or bars nearby. Parking is free, but limited during peak hours, so it's best to arrive early.

Best Time to Visit: If you're after a peaceful experience, avoid the high summer months and visit in May, June, or September. The quieter months also provide more opportunities to explore the surrounding nature.

Opening Times: Punta Bajlo is open year-round, though the best time to visit is from late spring to early autumn.

Address: Punta Bajlo, Zadar, Croatia

Borik Beach – Perfect for Families & Water Sports

Borik Beach is one of the most popular family-friendly beaches in Zadar, located about 4 km north of the city center. This spacious beach is ideal for families, offering shallow waters, a sandy seabed, and a variety of activities to keep both kids and adults entertained.

What to Expect: Borik Beach is well-developed with plenty of amenities, including rental kiosks for water sports like jet skiing, paddleboarding, and banana boat rides. The beach is primarily pebbled, but there are also sections with a sandy bottom, perfect for little ones. The water is calm, and the beach gradually deepens, making it safe for swimming. There are also plenty of sunbeds, umbrellas, and a number of cafes and restaurants where you can grab a meal or a cold drink.

For those who enjoy a more active beach day, Borik Beach has a volleyball court and is close to the **Bonači Water Sports Center**, where you can rent equipment for water activities.

Cost: Entrance to the beach is free, but rentals for water sports can range from $20-50 USD per hour, depending on the activity. Sunbeds cost around $10

USD per day, and cafes and restaurants offer meals and drinks starting at $5-10 USD.

Best Time to Visit: Borik is a popular spot, especially during the summer months. For the best experience, visit early in the morning or later in the afternoon to avoid the crowds. Spring and early autumn are ideal for a more relaxed visit.

Opening Times: The beach is open year-round, though the cafes and water sports centers operate primarily from May to October.

Address: Borik Beach, Zadar, Croatia

Saharun Beach (Dugi Otok) – Paradise Just a Ferry Ride Away

For those who are looking to escape the crowds and experience some of the best beaches in Croatia, **Saharun Beach** on **Dugi Otok** is a must-visit. This stunning beach is located on the northern coast of the island, just a short ferry ride from Zadar. Known for its white sand and turquoise waters, Saharun offers a true tropical beach experience without the long travel times to more distant locations.

What to Expect: Saharun Beach is a large, sandy beach surrounded by pine forests, which provide natural shade. The beach is perfect for swimming, sunbathing, and relaxing with a book, and the waters are incredibly clear. There are a few cafes and restaurants where you can enjoy fresh seafood and local delicacies, and the atmosphere is laid-back and peaceful.

You can rent a bike or scooter on the island to explore some of the nearby hidden coves or take a boat tour around Dugi Otok. Dugi Otok is also home to some excellent hiking trails, which provide stunning views of the Adriatic Sea.

Cost: Ferry tickets to Dugi Otok cost around $5-10 USD each way. There is no entrance fee for Saharun Beach, but rentals for umbrellas and sunbeds cost around $10 USD per day. A meal at one of the beachside restaurants typically costs around $15-25 USD.

Best Time to Visit: Visit in late spring or early autumn for the best weather and fewer tourists. During summer, the beach can get crowded, so it's ideal to visit in the morning or late afternoon.

Opening Times: Saharun Beach is open year-round, with ferry services running from April to October.

Address: Saharun Beach, Dugi Otok, Croatia

Ferry Information: Ferries from Zadar to Dugi Otok depart from the **Zadar Ferry Terminal**.

Queen's Beach (Nin) – Famous for Its Healing Mud

Located just 20 minutes from Zadar, **Queen's Beach** in **Nin** is famous not only for its natural beauty but also for its therapeutic mud, believed to have healing properties for skin conditions and joint pain. This sandy beach is a perfect blend of relaxation and wellness, making it a top choice for both locals and tourists.

What to Expect: Queen's Beach is a long stretch of sand with shallow, warm waters and soft, golden sand. The unique aspect of this beach is the mud, which is found in certain areas of the beach. The mud is rich in minerals, and visitors can coat themselves with it and leave it to dry in the sun before rinsing off in the sea. This treatment is said to be beneficial for skin and muscle ailments.

Besides the mud therapy, Queen's Beach is perfect for a leisurely swim, a walk along the shoreline, or just lounging in the sun. There are also restaurants nearby where you can try local dishes, particularly fresh seafood.

Cost: Access to the beach is free, but you'll find small kiosks selling mud for around $3-5 USD per container. Rentals for sunbeds cost around $10 USD per day, and a meal at a nearby restaurant typically costs $15-20 USD.

Best Time to Visit: Queen's Beach is best visited in late spring or early autumn, as the temperatures are perfect for enjoying the beach without the summer crowds.

Opening Times: The beach is open year-round, but the mud treatments are most popular from May to September.

Address: Queen's Beach, Nin, Zadar County, Croatia

8

What to Eat

& Drink in Zadar

A Culinary Journey Through Croatia's Historic Heart

Zadar, perched on the breathtaking Adriatic coast, is not only a city rich in history but also a haven for food lovers. As a local, I've spent years savoring the diverse flavors of the region, from traditional Dalmatian dishes to contemporary takes on local specialties. Whether you're a foodie in search of authentic flavors or just looking for a casual bite, Zadar offers a variety of culinary experiences. Here's a guide to what you *must* try during your visit.

Dalmatian Cuisine 101: What You Must Try

Dalmatian cuisine, the heart and soul of Zadar's food scene, is all about simplicity, quality ingredients, and traditional cooking methods passed down through generations. In Zadar, you'll taste the region's Mediterranean influences, which blend the fresh flavors of the sea with locally grown vegetables, olives, and herbs. Dishes are often grilled or roasted to perfection, and the focus is on fresh, seasonal ingredients.

Must-Try Dishes:

- **Pašticada**: A slow-cooked beef stew marinated in wine, vinegar, and spices, traditionally served with gnocchi or homemade pasta. It's rich, flavorful, and the perfect comfort food after a day of sightseeing.

- **Crni Rizot (Black Risotto)**: A squid ink risotto, rich and velvety with a distinctly oceanic flavor.

- **Grilled Fish**: Given Zadar's proximity to the sea, the fish here is fresh daily, often simply grilled with olive oil, garlic, and rosemary.

Where to Try It: Some of Zadar's best Dalmatian restaurants include **Konoba Didov San** and **Restaurant 4 Kantuna**, both offering a range of authentic Dalmatian dishes. Expect to pay about $15-25 USD per person for a hearty meal at these spots.

Average Price: Most Dalmatian dishes in Zadar will range between $12-30 USD depending on the restaurant. Prices are slightly higher at more upscale venues or beachfront restaurants.

Seafood Specialties – From Octopus Salad to Grilled Fish

Seafood is a cornerstone of Zadar's culinary identity, and the Adriatic Sea offers some of the freshest catch in the region. Whether you're craving octopus, sardines, or Mediterranean-style grilled fish, you'll find an abundance of seafood restaurants serving local specialties.

What to Try:

- **Salata od Hobotnice (Octopus Salad)**: A must-try for any seafood lover, this dish features tender, marinated octopus mixed with olive oil, garlic, and herbs, often served chilled. It's a refreshing starter or side dish.

- **Grilled Fish**: Zadar is known for its **Orada** (sea bream) and **Brancin** (sea bass), which are grilled to perfection with simple seasonings to enhance the natural flavors.

- **Sardines**: A common delicacy along the Dalmatian coast, these small fish are often grilled whole and served with a drizzle of olive oil and a squeeze of lemon.

Where to Try It:

- **Foša**: Situated right by the harbor, this restaurant offers incredible seafood dishes with fresh, local fish and seafood at affordable prices.

- **Pet Bunara**: This family-run gem serves fresh, Mediterranean seafood, and the **octopus salad** here is especially popular. A full meal including starters and main dishes typically costs around $25-35 USD per person.

Average Price: Expect to pay $15-30 USD for seafood dishes, depending on the restaurant and the catch of the day.

Peka (Slow-Cooked Meat & Seafood) – A Traditional Must-Try

If you want to experience a true Croatian culinary tradition, you have to try **Peka**. This dish involves slow-cooking meat (usually lamb, pork, or veal) and seafood with vegetables under a bell-shaped lid, which is placed over a fire and covered with embers. The slow cooking method results in incredibly tender and flavorful dishes.

What to Try:

- **Peka with Lamb**: Traditionally, it's prepared with lamb, which absorbs the smoky flavors from the slow-cooking process, becoming fall-apart tender.

- **Peka with Seafood**: This variation incorporates fish, shellfish, and sometimes octopus, all cooked to perfection under the lid.

Where to Try It:

- **Konoba Malo Misto**: Located just outside the city center, this cozy spot is known for its amazing Peka dishes. You can order Peka in advance, as it takes several hours to prepare.

- **Konoba Šime**: Situated a bit outside Zadar, this authentic restaurant offers both meat and seafood Peka, cooked to traditional standards. Expect to pay around $35-50 USD per person for a full Peka meal.

Average Price: A traditional Peka meal can cost anywhere from $25-40 USD, depending on the type of meat or seafood used.

Pag Cheese & Prosciutto – The Best Local Bites

No visit to Zadar would be complete without tasting **Pag Cheese** (Paški Sir) and **Prosciutto** (Pršut), two of Croatia's most beloved products. Pag, an island just a short drive from Zadar, is famous for its sheep milk cheese, which is rich, aromatic, and often served with a side of cured ham.

What to Try:

- **Paški Sir (Pag Cheese):** This cheese is made from sheep's milk, aged for several months, and has a distinctive, sharp flavor. It's often served as an appetizer or paired with bread, olives, and wine.

- **Pršut (Prosciutto):** The dry-cured ham is a staple in Dalmatian cuisine, usually served thinly sliced. Its salty, savory flavor pairs perfectly with cheese and local bread.

Where to Try It:

- **Zadar's Central Market:** You can pick up fresh Pag cheese and Prosciutto from local stalls in the city's central market, where the producers often sell directly to customers.

- **Konoba Tarsa:** For a more upscale experience, try **Konoba Tarsa**, where these delicacies are served with a glass of local wine.

Average Price: Expect to pay $8-15 USD for a plate of cheese and prosciutto, depending on the quality and the venue.

Maraschino Liqueur – Zadar's Signature Drink

Zadar is the birthplace of **Maraschino Liqueur**, a sweet cherry liqueur made from Marasca cherries, a variety indigenous to the region. This drink has been produced in Zadar since the 16th century and remains a beloved local specialty.

What to Try:

- **Maraschino Liqueur**: You'll find Maraschino served as a standalone shot, mixed in cocktails, or used in desserts. The liqueur is both sweet and slightly tart, making it incredibly refreshing.

- **Maraschino Cocktail**: A popular local twist involves mixing the liqueur with a splash of soda or tonic for a refreshing summer drink.

Where to Try It:

- **Maraschino Museum**: To learn more about the history of this iconic drink, visit the **Maraschino Museum** in the center of Zadar. The museum offers a taste of the liqueur and explains its production process. You can also purchase bottles to take home.

- **Café 4**: A popular café in Zadar that serves cocktails made with Maraschino. A typical cocktail here will cost around $6-8 USD.

Average Price: A shot of Maraschino will cost around $3-5 USD, while cocktails made with Maraschino typically range from $6-10 USD.

Where to Find the Best Gelato & Coffee

No culinary tour of Zadar is complete without indulging in some **gelato** or **coffee**. The city has a strong café culture, and many of the gelato shops serve high-quality, artisanal ice cream.

What to Try:

- **Gelato**: Flavors range from classic chocolate and vanilla to more unique local varieties, such as fig and olive oil.

- **Coffee**: Croatian coffee is strong and typically served as an espresso or black coffee. Many locals enjoy their coffee with a small pastry, like a **kolač** (cake).

Where to Try It:

- **Gelateria Caffe Bar**: Known for its delicious gelato, this café offers an array of flavors made with local ingredients.

- **Café Al Pacino**: Situated along the waterfront, this café is a great spot to enjoy a cup of strong Croatian coffee while people-watching.

Average Price: Gelato typically costs $2-4 USD per scoop, while a coffee will usually run around $1-2 USD.

9

Best

Restaurants, Cafés & Bars in Zadar

Where to Dine, Drink, and Unwind

Zadar's vibrant culinary scene combines fresh Mediterranean ingredients with Dalmatian traditions and a cosmopolitan flair. As a local, I can tell you that the city offers a wide range of dining options, from sophisticated fine dining experiences to casual, authentic eateries. Whether you're in the mood for an intimate dinner, a lively bar scene, or a perfect spot to sip coffee by the sea, Zadar has it all. Here's a comprehensive guide to the best restaurants, cafés, and bars in the city, with practical tips on what to expect and how to make the most of your experience.

Fine Dining & Romantic Spots

Foša ($$$) – Waterfront Elegance

Address: Obala kralja Petra Krešimira IV 4, 23000 Zadar

Phone: +385 23 342 002

Website: fosa.hr

Opening Hours: Daily, 12:00 PM – 11:00 PM

If you're looking for an elegant dining experience with a stunning waterfront view, **Foša** is one of Zadar's best fine-dining restaurants. Located by the old harbor, this restaurant offers an idyllic setting where you can enjoy Mediterranean delicacies and freshly prepared seafood. The dining room is tastefully designed, with a blend of contemporary and traditional elements that reflect the timeless beauty of Zadar.

Foša is known for its exquisite seafood dishes, particularly **grilled fish**, **scallops**, and **tuna tartare**, all of which highlight the freshest catches from the Adriatic Sea. For those who enjoy a more refined dining experience, **Foša's tasting menu** is an exceptional way to explore the flavors of Dalmatia, with courses expertly paired with local wines.

What to Try:

- **Tuna Tartare**: Light, fresh, and expertly balanced, it's a perfect start to your meal.

- **Grilled Sea Bass**: One of the best in town, prepared with minimal seasoning to let the quality of the fish shine.

- **Seafood Risotto**: Creamy, rich, and packed with a variety of fresh seafood.

Average Price: Expect to pay around $45-65 USD per person for a full meal, including a starter, main course, and dessert.

Pet Bunara ($$$) – Farm-to-Table Delights

Address: Šimunovo polje 2, 23000 Zadar

Phone: +385 23 213 672

Website: petbunara.hr

Opening Hours: Monday – Saturday, 12:00 PM – 11:00 PM; Closed on Sundays

For a truly authentic Dalmatian experience, **Pet Bunara** brings the farm-to-table concept to Zadar with a focus on locally sourced, seasonal ingredients. The restaurant is nestled in a rustic stone house, offering an intimate, cozy atmosphere perfect for a romantic dinner. Their dishes change frequently depending on what's in season, so there's always something new to try.

Their signature dish is **slow-cooked lamb**, prepared with a variety of fresh herbs and served alongside roasted vegetables. **Homemade pastas** and **cheese platters** are also popular, and the wine list, curated to feature the best of Croatian wineries, complements the meal perfectly.

What to Try:

- **Lamb Peka**: A must-try for anyone visiting, the tender lamb is cooked slowly in an underground oven, a classic Dalmatian preparation.

- **Homemade Pasticada**: A rich beef stew served with gnocchi, packed with flavor and slow-cooked for hours.

- **Local Cheese Platter**: An excellent way to sample some of the finest cheeses from Zadar and the surrounding region.

Average Price: A meal here typically costs around $40-60 USD per person, depending on your choices.

Casual & Authentic Croatian Eateries

Konoba Skoblar ($$) – Traditional Dalmatian Tavern

Address: Ulica Klementa 2, 23000 Zadar

Phone: +385 23 343 703

Opening Hours: Tuesday – Sunday, 12:00 PM – 11:00 PM; Closed on Mondays

Located in the heart of Zadar, **Konoba Skoblar** is a quintessential Dalmatian tavern that provides an authentic, no-frills dining experience. The atmosphere is rustic and warm, with exposed stone walls and wooden beams, and the food is straightforward and delicious. This is a place where locals love to gather for hearty meals after a long day.

The menu features a selection of grilled meats, fresh seafood, and traditional **Dalmatian-style appetizers** like **marinated anchovies** and **olive**

tapenade. The portions are generous, and the prices are very reasonable considering the quality of the food.

What to Try:

- **Grilled Octopus**: Tender and smoky, this is a simple yet satisfying dish that showcases the quality of local seafood.

- **Buzara**: A popular Dalmatian dish made with seafood, typically shellfish, cooked in white wine, garlic, and olive oil.

- **Ćevapi**: Small, flavorful sausages that are often served with flatbread and fresh onions.

Average Price: A full meal at Konoba Skoblar will cost around $20-30 USD per person.

Bruschetta ($$) – Italian & Mediterranean Fusion

Address: Ulica Miha Pracata 10, 23000 Zadar

Phone: +385 23 310 100

Opening Hours: Daily, 12:00 PM – 11:00 PM

If you're in the mood for something with a twist, **Bruschetta** offers a unique fusion of Italian and Mediterranean flavors. This charming eatery, with its warm, inviting ambiance, specializes in freshly made **pasta**, **wood-fired pizzas**, and Mediterranean seafood dishes. It's perfect for casual dining with a modern flair.

The standout dish at Bruschetta is their **seafood pasta**, which is loaded with fresh shellfish, clams, and mussels, all served in a rich, flavorful tomato sauce. The **pizza** is also a favorite, with a perfectly crisp crust and a wide variety of toppings.

What to Try:

- **Seafood Risotto**: Another local specialty that features the bounty of the Adriatic, rich with seafood and perfectly creamy.

- **Wood-Fired Pizza**: With toppings like fresh mozzarella, anchovies, and olives, it's the perfect choice for a light yet satisfying meal.

- **Homemade Gnocchi**: Pillowy soft and served with a variety of sauces, it's a perfect way to enjoy Italian-inspired Dalmatian cooking.

Average Price: Expect to pay around $20-30 USD for a main course at Bruschetta.

Best Local Cafés & Bakeries

Kavana Lovre – Iconic Café in the Old Town

Address: Narodni Trg 2, 23000 Zadar
Phone: +385 23 313 092
Opening Hours: Daily, 7:30 AM – 11:00 PM

No visit to Zadar is complete without stopping by **Kavana Lovre**, an iconic café located in the heart of the Old Town, right on the main square. This charming café is a local institution, known for its excellent coffee and delightful pastries. The outdoor seating offers a perfect vantage point for people-watching while sipping a cup of strong espresso.

What to Try:

- **Croatian Pastries**: Sample a selection of freshly baked local pastries, including **kolači** (cakes) and **burek** (savory pastry filled with meat or cheese).

- **Coffee**: The café serves excellent espresso, as well as a variety of other coffee options like macchiatos and cappuccinos.

Average Price: Coffee here costs about $2-3 USD, while pastries are priced at $1-2 USD.

Art Kavana – Trendy & Artsy Vibes

Address: Ulica Andrije Kačića Miošića 2, 23000 Zadar

Phone: +385 23 235 365

Opening Hours: Daily, 8:00 AM – 10:00 PM

For a more artsy and contemporary vibe, head to **Art Kavana**, an eclectic café that doubles as an art gallery. The décor is modern and stylish, with rotating exhibitions from local artists. It's a great place to enjoy a cup of coffee while appreciating the creativity around you.

What to Try:

- **Iced Coffee**: Perfect for a warm afternoon, served with a scoop of ice cream for a sweet treat.

- **Sweet Pastries**: Try the **apple strudel** or **chocolate croissants**.

Average Price: Expect to pay around $3-5 USD for a coffee, and $2-3 USD for a pastry.

Rooftop Bars & Sunset Cocktails

The Garden Lounge – Laid-Back Lounge with a View

Address: Ulica Ivana Mažuranića 1, 23000 Zadar

Phone: +385 98 990 1104

Opening Hours: Daily, 5:00 PM – Late

For an unforgettable sunset cocktail with panoramic views of the city and the sea, **The Garden Lounge** is a must-visit. Perched above Zadar, this rooftop bar provides a laid-back atmosphere, perfect for sipping a signature cocktail while enjoying the view. It's a popular spot for both locals and tourists looking to unwind after a busy day.

What to Try:

- **Garden Spritz**: Their take on the classic Aperol Spritz, light and refreshing.

- **Gin & Tonic**: A local favorite, with a wide variety of gin options.

Average Price: Expect to pay around $8-12 USD for a cocktail.

Ledana Lounge & Bar – Chic Nightlife Spot

Address: Ulica Josipa Jurja Strossmayera 1, 23000 Zadar

Phone: +385 98 213 400

Opening Hours: Thursday – Saturday, 9:00 PM – Late

If you're looking to dance and enjoy a more vibrant nightlife scene, **Ledana Lounge & Bar** is the place to be. This chic lounge and bar offer a variety of cocktails, an extensive wine list, and an electric atmosphere, making it a perfect spot to dance the night away.

What to Try:

- **Signature Cocktails**: Ledana is known for its expertly crafted cocktails, including the **Ledana Mule** and **Passionfruit Martini**.

Average Price: Expect to pay around $10-15 USD for a cocktail.

10 Outdoor

Adventures & Activities in Zadar

*Z*adar is the perfect base for outdoor adventurers seeking an unforgettable blend of coastline, pristine islands, and nature-packed landscapes. Whether you're a water sports enthusiast, a hiker, or someone looking for a rush of adrenaline, the region offers something for everyone. From kayaking in crystal-clear waters to scaling mountain trails, Zadar guarantees a thrilling outdoor experience. Here's your ultimate guide to the top outdoor adventures and activities to enjoy in Zadar, with details on the best spots, how to get the most out of your visit, and average costs.

Kayaking & Stand-Up Paddleboarding Around the Islands

One of the best ways to experience the stunning beauty of Zadar's coastline is by getting out on the water. Kayaking and Stand-Up Paddleboarding (SUP) are fantastic activities to explore Zadar's crystal-clear waters, and the nearby islands offer a serene yet thrilling backdrop.

Where to Go:
The nearby **Dugi Otok** (Long Island) is a perfect destination for both kayaking and paddleboarding. The **Sakarun Beach** area on Dugi Otok, with its turquoise waters, is especially popular among kayakers. If you're new to the sport, there are plenty of **kayak and SUP rentals** in Zadar town. **Zadar Kayak Tours** (located at the Zadar Marina) offers guided tours that take you along the coastline and to nearby islets like **Ladesta**.

Cost:
Renting a single kayak or SUP typically costs around $15-25 USD per hour. Guided group tours can range from $40-60 USD per person, which usually lasts 2-3 hours. If you prefer a private tour, expect to pay about $70-100 USD.

What to Expect:
You'll glide through calm, crystal-clear waters while taking in the scenic beauty of Zadar's coastal islands, including **Ugljan** and **Pasman**. For those seeking an extra challenge, try paddling along the rugged coastline of **Vrgada Island**, which features small coves and natural caves to explore.

Best   Time   to   Go:
The summer months (June to September) are ideal for kayaking and paddleboarding, but early mornings or late afternoons will give you the calmest waters and fewer crowds.

Helpful   Tip:
If you plan to rent a kayak or SUP, be sure to check the condition of the equipment and confirm that the rental fee includes safety gear like a life vest. Many rental places also offer discounts for full-day rentals or group bookings.

Scuba Diving & Snorkeling: Discovering Zadar's Underwater World

Zadar's coastline is not only rich in history but also teeming with marine life. Its clear waters are perfect for exploring the underwater world, whether you're an experienced diver or a first-time snorkeler.

Where   to   Dive:
One of the best places for scuba diving near Zadar is **Vrgada Island**, known for its underwater caves,

drop-offs, and a variety of marine species. For beginners, the calm waters near **Ugljan Island** offer excellent shallow dive sites. Dive centers such as **Scuba Zadar** and **Diving Center Petrcane** offer both guided dives and snorkeling tours.

Cost:

A guided snorkeling tour typically costs around $30-50 USD per person, with equipment included. For certified divers, a single dive with equipment rental can range from $40-80 USD. Scuba diving courses for beginners start at $200-250 USD, which includes several days of training.

What   to   Expect:

Underwater, you'll be greeted by vibrant coral reefs, colorful fish, and occasionally even a friendly octopus or sea turtle. If you're diving near the **Zadar Channel**, the warm waters make for spectacular visibility and marine biodiversity.

Best   Time   to   Go:

The prime diving season in Zadar is from late spring to early autumn (May to October). During these months, visibility is at its best, and the water temperature is comfortable, usually ranging from 20-25°C (68-77°F).

Helpful   Tip:
For those new to diving, consider taking a PADI course or a "Discover Scuba Diving" session, which allows you to dive even without a certification. These courses can be found at most diving centers, and it's a great way to experience the underwater beauty in a safe, controlled environment.

Hiking & Cycling Routes Near Zadar

For those who prefer the ground beneath their feet (or the wheels beneath them), Zadar is surrounded by numerous trails offering panoramic views, rugged terrains, and a connection to nature.

Hiking   Trails:
The **Velebit Mountain Range**, a UNESCO Biosphere Reserve, offers some of Croatia's most stunning hiking routes. Trails like **Sveti Rok** and **Paklenica National Park** are ideal for both beginners and experienced trekkers, with well-marked

paths leading to breathtaking peaks. If you're looking for something closer, the **Zadar Hinterland** has more relaxed but equally scenic routes, offering views of the islands and Adriatic Sea.

Cycling   Routes:
Zadar is part of the Croatian cycling network, with routes ranging from leisurely rides to more intense challenges. The **Biciklistička Staza Zadar** (Zadar Cycling Route) takes you along the coast, passing through charming villages and offering plenty of photo opportunities. For mountain biking enthusiasts, the trails in **Paklenica** provide a more demanding ride through rocky terrain and forest paths.

Cost:
Cycling rentals typically cost around $15-25 USD per day. Guided biking tours around Zadar or to nearby islands range from $30-50 USD per person, with full-day tours priced between $70-90 USD.

What   to   Expect:
On foot or by bike, you'll be able to immerse yourself in the natural beauty of Zadar's surrounding areas. Expect magnificent coastal views, dense pine forests,

and Mediterranean flora. For an added challenge, consider cycling through the rugged terrain around **Telašćica Nature Park** on Dugi Otok.

Best Time to Go: Spring and autumn are the best times for hiking and cycling, as the weather is mild, and the trails are not overcrowded. Summer can be hot, so early mornings or late afternoons are ideal.

Helpful Tip: If you're cycling, make sure to wear a helmet and bring enough water, as the sun can get intense. Many local cycling tour operators provide high-quality mountain bikes, so it's worth checking the equipment before heading out.

Sailing & Boat Excursions

There's no better way to explore the beautiful coastline of Zadar and its islands than by boat. Zadar has a range of sailing and boat excursion options, from private charters to group tours.

Where to Sail:

A private sailing tour around the **Kornati Islands** is a bucket-list experience. The **Kornati National Park**, with its 150 islands, is a sailor's paradise, offering serene waters, secluded coves, and pristine beaches. For something shorter, a boat trip to **Ugljan Island** or **Silba Island** provides a taste of the Adriatic's beauty.

Cost:

Boat rentals range from $100-200 USD for a half-day tour, with private sailing trips costing anywhere from $300-600 USD for a full day, depending on the type of boat. Group tours are more affordable, often ranging from $40-70 USD per person.

What to Expect:

Sailing gives you a unique perspective of the coastline, with stops for swimming, snorkeling, and sunbathing on pristine beaches. Many boat excursions offer a meal on board, with freshly caught fish and local delicacies.

Best Time to Go:

The best sailing season is from late spring to early

autumn (May to September). The waters are calm, and the weather is perfect for a day on the sea.

Helpful **Tip**:
If you're not familiar with sailing, consider booking a skipper for your private charter. They'll not only navigate but can also take you to hidden spots around the islands that you might otherwise miss.

Paragliding & Skydiving Over the Adriatic

For the ultimate adrenaline rush, why not soar over Zadar? Paragliding and skydiving over the Adriatic offer a thrilling way to see the coastline from above, with panoramic views of the islands and the crystal-clear sea.

Where **to** **Go**:
Zadar Paragliding offers tandem paragliding flights, where you'll be strapped to an experienced pilot and glide over **Vrana Lake** or the coastline for about 20-30 minutes. For skydiving, **Skydive Croatia** operates out of Zadar Airport and offers breathtaking tandem

jumps, with views of the Adriatic, the islands, and the Dinaric Alps.

Cost:
Paragliding prices range from $90-150 USD per person for a tandem flight. Tandem skydiving experiences typically cost around $250-350 USD per jump.

What to Expect:
Paragliding offers a peaceful, scenic flight that lets you glide over picturesque landscapes. For skydiving, expect a thrilling freefall followed by a serene parachute descent, offering a completely different perspective of the Adriatic.

Best Time to Go:
The best time for paragliding and skydiving is from spring to early autumn, when the weather is calm and clear.

Helpful Tip:
Both activities require no prior experience, but it's essential to check the weather conditions in advance. These experiences are weather-dependent, so be

prepared for possible delays or rescheduling due to wind or cloud cover.

11 Zadar's

Festivals &

Events in 2025

A Vibrant Celebration of Culture, Music, and Traditions

Zadar, with its fascinating history and stunning coastal beauty, is not just a destination for sightseeing, but a city alive with culture, music, and celebrations throughout the year. Whether you're here for the electrifying music festivals, the magic of Christmas, or the creative energy of film lovers, Zadar hosts an impressive range of festivals and events that capture the spirit of this beautiful city. In 2025, the city promises to host several unforgettable festivals, each bringing its own flavor to the Adriatic shores. Let's dive into the most anticipated events in Zadar for 2025 and make sure you know how to make the most of them.

Zadar Sunset Festival – Music, DJs & Beach Vibes

The **Zadar Sunset Festival** is a must-visit for those seeking music, good vibes, and a breathtaking coastal setting. Held annually, the festival takes place in the summer months, typically between June and

September, transforming Zadar's coastline into a lively party hub. The festival's name perfectly captures the essence of what this event is all about: music, sunsets, and beach vibes.

Where It Takes Place: The festival is held along **Kolovare Beach** and at various other beach clubs and open-air venues across the city. Kolovare Beach, located just a short walk from Zadar's old town, offers incredible views of the sunset over the Adriatic Sea, making it the ideal spot for festival-goers.

What to Expect: Expect an eclectic mix of electronic dance music, house, techno, and some chill beats, as local and international DJs take to the stage and mix tunes from sunset to late into the night. The event has a relaxed yet vibrant atmosphere, with a range of food and drink vendors serving up local delicacies and cold beverages. Many festival-goers come here for the music, but also to soak in the beauty of Zadar's coastal views. The beach setting provides the perfect backdrop for an unforgettable festival experience.

Cost:

Tickets for the Zadar Sunset Festival generally range from $30-$60 USD, depending on the day or the lineup. VIP tickets for exclusive access areas or backstage passes can cost anywhere from $100 to $150 USD. Many of the beach parties are free to enter, although they may require a drink purchase to get in.

Best Time to Go:

If you want the full experience, come in July or August, when the festival's atmosphere is in full swing and the weather is warm enough to enjoy both the music and the sea.

How to Get the Most Out of It:

Make sure to arrive early for prime spots on the beach. Bring some comfortable shoes, as you'll likely be dancing on sand, and don't forget sunscreen. The festival stretches long into the evening, so consider staying nearby or booking a hotel with late-night access for convenience. If you're planning to stay in Zadar after the festival, hotels like **Falkensteiner Hotel & Spa Iadera** (a 5-star beachfront property) are ideal for unwinding after a night of partying.

Full Moon Festival – A Night Market by the Sea

One of the most unique experiences you'll have in Zadar is the **Full Moon Festival**, a cultural event that turns the city's waterfront into a magical night market. This festival is a must for anyone visiting in the summer, as it's all about local crafts, food, music, and the mesmerizing sight of the full moon rising over the sea.

Where It Takes Place: The event is primarily held at the **Zadar Waterfront**, stretching from the city's famous **Sea Organ** all the way to the **Greeting to the Sun** installation. These locations make the Full Moon Festival truly one of a kind, combining the natural beauty of the Adriatic coastline with a lively atmosphere. Visitors can enjoy the sunset, then linger as the full moon rises, all while perusing the market stalls or enjoying local delicacies.

What to Expect: At the Full Moon Festival, visitors can explore booths and stalls selling everything from handmade jewelry and local art to organic skincare products and traditional Croatian crafts. Expect local musicians to set the mood with live performances, and food vendors offering authentic street food such as **grilled fish**, **octopus salad**, and locally made **marzipan**. It's a celebration of local culture and community, with everyone coming together to celebrate the night in the glow of the full moon.

Cost:
Entrance is typically free, but food and drink prices will vary depending on what you're craving. Expect to pay $5-15 USD for a meal and around $3-5 USD for local beverages like **rakija** or a refreshing beer.

Best   Time   to   Go:
The Full Moon Festival usually takes place once a month, around the time of the full moon. Check the lunar calendar to time your visit to coincide with one of these enchanting nights. The summer months are the busiest, with plenty of events and festivities, but the atmosphere is relaxed and charming year-round.

How   to   Get   the   Most   Out   of   It:
To make the most of this event, plan to come early to explore the market, and don't forget to wander along the Sea Organ and Greeting to the Sun to experience

the magical atmosphere. Be sure to stay for the moonrise—it's a moment that will leave you in awe. Since it's a popular event, you might want to reserve a table at a nearby restaurant in advance if you want to enjoy dinner with a view.

Zadar Film Festival – For Movie Lovers & Creators

For cinephiles and aspiring filmmakers alike, the **Zadar Film Festival** is one of the highlights of the city's cultural calendar. Held every summer, usually in late June or early July, the festival attracts filmmakers, industry professionals, and movie lovers from around the world. It's a celebration of independent cinema, with a focus on creativity, storytelling, and the power of film to explore human experiences.

Where It Takes Place: The Zadar Film Festival is held in various venues around the city, but the primary screening locations are the **Zadar Cinema** (a modern venue in the city center) and outdoor screenings along the city walls, providing a truly unique cinematic experience. The outdoor screenings are particularly special, with the ancient city walls serving as a stunning backdrop to films.

What to Expect: The festival features a range of films, including short films, feature films, and documentaries. It showcases a mix of international and Croatian films, with a particular emphasis on up-and-coming filmmakers and fresh talent. In addition to the screenings, the festival often hosts panel discussions, Q&A sessions, and workshops for aspiring filmmakers. The atmosphere is welcoming, and there's a real sense of community as filmmakers engage with their audiences.

Cost:
Ticket prices vary depending on whether you're attending a screening, a workshop, or a panel discussion. Expect to pay around $7-15 USD for a single ticket to a film screening. Workshops or special events may range from $20-50 USD. Festival passes, which grant access to multiple events, can cost around $50-100 USD.

Best Time to Go: The festival typically runs for a week in late June or early July. If you're a movie lover or a filmmaker, plan ahead and purchase your tickets early to ensure you get the most out of this celebrated event.

How to Get the Most Out of It: Take the time to attend a variety of screenings, but also be sure to attend some of the post-screening discussions with filmmakers to gain insight into the creative process. Zadar itself has a rich history in film, and the city's ancient walls and stunning coastal views provide the perfect setting for both the films and the audiences.

Advent in Zadar – A Magical Christmas Experience

If you find yourself in Zadar during the holiday season, be sure to visit **Advent in Zadar**, the city's magical Christmas market and celebration. From late November to early January, Zadar's old town transforms into a winter wonderland, where visitors can immerse themselves in the festive spirit with lights, music, and delicious local treats.

Where It Takes Place: The Advent celebrations take place throughout the Old Town, with the focal point being the **People's Square** (Narodni Trg). The entire town square is lit up with festive lights, and the market is dotted with charming wooden stalls selling local crafts, hot drinks, and seasonal food.

What to Expect: Advent in Zadar offers something for everyone, from traditional Croatian Christmas food like **fritule** (fried dough balls) and **kuhani vin** (mulled wine) to hand-crafted gifts. There are plenty of activities for families, including an ice skating rink and live performances by local choirs. The festivities culminate with a special **New Year's Eve celebration**, where people gather by the sea to welcome in the New Year.

Cost: Entry to the Christmas market is free, but food and drinks are priced at $3-8 USD per item. Ice skating typically costs around $5-8 USD for a session. Special performances or events may have a small entry fee of $10-20 USD.

Best Time to Go: The Advent festivities start in late November and continue until early January, with the peak of the celebrations occurring around **Christmas Eve** and **New Year's Eve**.

How to Get the Most Out of It: Make sure to try local holiday treats, stroll around the beautifully decorated streets, and enjoy the festive atmosphere. If you're planning to visit Advent in Zadar, be sure to book your accommodation in advance, as this is a popular time to visit the city. Hotels such as **Hotel Bastion** or **Heritage Hotel** offer cozy settings and are within walking distance of all the Advent festivities.

12 Shopping & Souvenirs in Zadar

Zadar, Croatia, is not just a city brimming with rich history and breathtaking landscapes, it's also a wonderful place to shop. From handcrafted jewelry to fresh produce and traditional Croatian wines, Zadar offers an array of shopping experiences that will allow you to take a piece of this enchanting city home with you. Whether you're looking for authentic souvenirs or just want to explore local markets, there's something for every taste and budget. In this guide, I'll walk you through some of the best places to shop in Zadar, sharing details, average prices, and tips for getting the most out of your shopping experience.

Handmade Jewelry & Local Crafts

Zadar is a haven for artisans who take pride in their craft, and you'll find numerous shops offering beautiful, handmade jewelry and local crafts. From silver earrings to leather goods, handmade items capture the essence of Croatian culture and make perfect keepsakes from your travels.

Where to Buy:

- **Bastion Crafts & Jewelry** (Located in the heart of Zadar's Old Town, near the Roman Forum) is an excellent place to start. Known for its collection of silver and gemstone jewelry, you'll find unique pieces inspired by Croatian history and nature. Prices here typically range from $20 to $150 USD, depending on the intricacy of the designs and materials used.

- **Zadar Art & Craft Center** (Located on Široka Ulica, Zadar's main pedestrian street) features a selection of hand-crafted products, including intricate jewelry, scarves, ceramics, and wooden crafts. Prices for jewelry range from $15 to $75 USD, and ceramics start at about $10 USD for small decorative pieces.

- **Zadar Artisan Shop** (Located on Kalelarga Street) focuses on local craftsmanship and offers everything from ceramics to hand-painted tiles. Expect to pay around $10 for a small hand-painted tile or $50 for a more elaborate ceramic vase.

Getting the Most Out of It: When shopping for jewelry and crafts, ask the artisans about the inspiration behind their work. Many pieces are inspired by the natural beauty of Zadar and the surrounding Adriatic coastline. Don't be afraid to negotiate prices, especially for higher-priced items. Many local shops offer discounts if you purchase multiple items.

Opening Times: Most shops in the Old Town open daily from 9:00 AM to 7:00 PM, though some may close for lunch between 1:00 PM and 3:00 PM. Make sure to check the hours in advance if you're going closer to closing time.

Best Markets for Fresh Produce & Local Specialties

Zadar is a city that thrives on fresh, local produce, and there's no better place to experience this than its bustling markets. Whether you're looking for fruits, vegetables, homemade olive oil, or local honey, the markets of Zadar offer an authentic taste of the region.

Where to Buy:

- **Zadar's Green Market (Tržnica)** (Located near the Old Town at Ul. Stjepana Radića) is the city's main open-air market and a must-visit for anyone wanting to experience the flavors of Zadar. Here, you'll find an abundance of fresh fruit, vegetables, herbs, and flowers. Expect to pay about $1-$3 USD for a bag of fresh produce like tomatoes, figs, and olives, while a liter of olive oil will cost around $8-$12 USD, depending on the quality and producer.

- **Fish Market (Ribarnica)** (Located near the Green Market at Obala kralja Tomislava) is a paradise for seafood lovers. Fresh fish such as anchovies, tuna, and sea bass are sold daily, and if you're keen to try local delicacies, you can buy octopus and shellfish. Prices for fresh fish range from $5 to $15 USD per kilo, depending on the type of fish.

- **Petra's Organic Market** (Located on the outskirts of Zadar, in the town of Petrčane) is the perfect spot for organic goods. You'll find a variety of fresh herbs, farm-fresh eggs, and seasonal vegetables. Expect to pay around $10-$20 USD for a basket full of organic produce.

Getting the Most Out of It: For the freshest produce and the best deals, visit the markets early in the morning before the crowds arrive. It's also the best time to interact with local vendors and ask for recommendations. Don't forget to sample some of the delicious local olive oils, cheeses, and homemade jams—they're all available at the market and make great souvenirs. If you're looking for unique edible gifts to bring home, the Green Market offers small, beautifully wrapped packs of dried herbs or locally made honey.

Opening Times: The Green Market and Fish Market are open from 6:00 AM to 2:00 PM, Monday to Saturday, but they may close earlier on Saturdays. The Petra's Organic Market has more limited hours, typically open on weekends from 9:00 AM to 3:00 PM.

Where to Buy Pag Cheese & Dalmatian Wines

No trip to Zadar would be complete without tasting the famous **Pag cheese** and the wines from the surrounding Dalmatian region. Luckily, these delicious products are readily available for purchase throughout the city.

Where to Buy:

- **Zadar Wine Shop (Vinoteka Zadar)** (Located at Obala kneza Branimira 8) is a great spot to pick up local wines. The shop specializes in Dalmatian wines, including the popular **Plavac Mali**, **Pošip**, and **Žlahtina** varieties. Wine prices start around $10 per bottle for a basic local wine and go up to $40+ for premium bottles from boutique wineries.

- **Pag Cheese Store** (Located in Zadar's Old Town, near the Cathedral of St. Anastasia) is the best place to find the famous **Paški Sir**, a sheep's milk cheese from the island of Pag. A 200g wheel of Pag cheese can cost anywhere from $10 to $20 USD, depending on the age and quality of the cheese. The cheese is rich, salty, and perfect with a glass of wine.

- **Trg 4 (Pag Cheese Market)** (Located in the Old Town) offers a wide range of local specialties, including dried meats and Pag cheese. Prices for Pag cheese can range from $15 to $30 per kilo, depending on the age.

Getting the Most Out of It: To get the most out of your wine and cheese shopping experience, ask the vendors for tasting recommendations. Many of the wine shops and Pag cheese stores will let you sample before you buy. For Pag cheese, ask for suggestions on how best to pair it with wine or traditional Dalmatian breads. Consider purchasing a bottle of wine and some cheese as a gift for someone back home, as these are truly authentic Croatian delicacies.

Opening Times: Most wine shops and cheese stores are open daily from 9:00 AM to 7:00 PM, though they may close a little earlier in the off-season months.

Art Galleries & Unique Finds

If you're looking for more artistic souvenirs or just want to browse the local art scene, Zadar has a great selection of galleries showcasing the work of Croatian artists. Whether you're in the market for a painting, sculpture, or handmade textiles, you'll find plenty of unique pieces.

Where to Buy:

- **Museum of Ancient Glass Gift Shop** (Located at Trg Tri Bunara 1) features an exquisite collection of handmade glassworks and art inspired by Zadar's rich history. Here, you can buy glass jewelry, sculptures, and decorative items. Prices for small glass items range from $10 to $50 USD.

- **Art Gallery Zadar** (Located at Ul. Jurja Barakovića 8) is known for showcasing contemporary Croatian art. Expect to find paintings, prints, and sculptures by local artists. Prices for original works of art can range from

$100 to $1000 USD, depending on the artist and medium.

- **Galerija Galiot** (Located on Ulica Filipa Benkovića) is another top gallery in Zadar, specializing in paintings, drawings, and sculptures by Croatian and international artists. Here, you can find unique souvenirs such as hand-painted ceramics and pottery, with prices ranging from $30 to $150 USD.

Getting the Most Out of It: Take time to chat with the gallery owners and artists themselves. Many local artists are more than happy to share the story behind their work, which makes for an even more meaningful souvenir. If you're visiting a gallery, be sure to ask if they offer a certificate of authenticity or an artist's bio to accompany your purchase.

Opening Times: Most galleries are open daily from 10:00 AM to 6:00 PM, although some may close on Sundays or during holidays. It's always a good idea to check the gallery's schedule before planning your visit.

13 Essential

Travel Tips & Practical Info for Zadar

Zadar is a city brimming with history, culture, and stunning natural beauty, making it a top destination for travelers seeking a true Adriatic experience. However, to fully enjoy what this beautiful Croatian gem has to offer, it's essential to be well-prepared. From the best time to visit, language tips, and currency insights, to the essentials of health, safety, and connectivity, this guide provides practical tips to help you make the most out of your trip to Zadar.

Best Time to Visit Zadar – Seasonal Pros & Cons

Zadar enjoys a Mediterranean climate, which means hot summers, mild winters, and plenty of sunshine throughout the year. However, the best time to visit depends on what you're hoping to experience during your trip. Let's take a look at the pros and cons of visiting during each season.

Spring (April - June)

- **Pros**: This is arguably the best time to visit Zadar. The weather is pleasant, with average temperatures ranging from 15°C (59°F) to 25°C

(77°F), making it ideal for sightseeing and outdoor activities. The tourist crowds are still relatively thin, meaning you can enjoy popular attractions like the Sea Organ or Roman Forum without feeling overcrowded. Spring also marks the beginning of the festival season, and you can catch some of the smaller, local cultural events.

- **Cons**: The sea may still be a bit cold for swimming, though the weather is warm enough to enjoy outdoor cafes and walks along the coast.

- **Average Costs**: Accommodations in Zadar during spring are generally more affordable than in peak summer, with hotel prices ranging from $80 to $200 per night depending on the area and star rating.

Summer (July - August)

- **Pros**: This is the high season in Zadar. The Adriatic Sea is at its warmest, ideal for swimming, beach activities, and boat excursions. Zadar's lively summer festivals, including the famous **Zadar Sunset Festival**, are in full swing, with vibrant nightlife and plenty of events. Expect long sunny days, perfect for exploring the city's charming Old Town, the Sea Organ, and the surrounding islands.

- **Cons**: Zadar can become quite crowded with tourists, especially in July and August, which means higher prices for accommodation, meals, and excursions. The heat can be intense, with temperatures often soaring above 30°C (86°F), making it less comfortable for sightseeing, especially during midday.

- **Average Costs**: Expect peak-season prices with accommodation rates ranging from $100 to $300 per night at mid-range hotels. Popular tours and activities also tend to be pricier in the summer months.

Autumn (September - October)

- **Pros**: Autumn in Zadar offers a pleasant blend of warm weather and fewer crowds. Temperatures are still comfortable, hovering between 20°C (68°F) and 25°C (77°F), making it great for exploring the city, hiking, or enjoying the coastline. The grape harvest season also means that many wineries offer wine-tasting tours, and local festivals continue well into September.

- **Cons**: The weather can be unpredictable at times, with occasional rainfall. However, it's still warm enough for beach days and outdoor dining.

- **Average Costs**: Prices for accommodation in autumn are lower than summer rates, with a good range of options available for $75 to $150 per night.

Winter (November - March)

- **Pros**: If you prefer a quiet, more intimate experience, winter in Zadar is perfect. The city is peaceful and free from the typical tourist crowds, and the weather is mild enough for walking around the Old Town and enjoying the city's historical sites. Plus, you can get great deals on accommodations during this off-season period.

- **Cons**: The weather can be cold and rainy, with temperatures ranging from 5°C (41°F) to 15°C (59°F). The sea is too cold for swimming, and some tours and activities may be limited due to the off-season.

- **Average Costs**: Winter is the best time for budget travelers, as hotel rates can be as low as $50 to $100 per night.

Language Tips: Croatian Phrases Every Traveler Should Know

Croatian is the official language in Zadar, but English is widely spoken, especially in the touristy areas. Still, learning a few key phrases in Croatian can go a long way in making a positive impression on the locals.

Useful Phrases:

- **Hello** – *Bok* (informal) or *Dobar dan* (formal)

- **Goodbye** – *Doviđenja*

- **Please** – *Molim*

- **Thank you** – *Hvala*

- **Yes** – *Da*

- **No** – *Ne*

- **How much is this?** – *Koliko ovo košta?*

- **Where is the bathroom?** – *Gdje je WC?*

- **I don't understand** – *Ne razumijem*

It's always appreciated when travelers make an effort to speak the local language, even if it's just a few words. The locals will usually respond in English if needed, but your efforts will make them feel more comfortable and respected.

Currency, ATMs & Paying by Card

Zadar, like the rest of Croatia, uses the **Croatian kuna (HRK)** as its currency. While Croatia is working towards adopting the Euro, the kuna remains the official currency for now.

- **Currency Exchange**: There are plenty of currency exchange offices around the Old Town, though they often charge a commission. For the best rates, use ATMs to withdraw cash directly. You'll usually find ATMs at the airport, near major tourist spots, and inside shopping malls.

- **Paying by Card**: Credit and debit cards are widely accepted in hotels, restaurants, and shops. Visa and MasterCard are the most commonly accepted, though it's always a good idea to carry some cash for smaller establishments, markets, or taxis.

- **Average Costs**: At most cafes and restaurants, meals range from $8 to $25 USD, depending on the location and type of cuisine. When paying with a card, you may be asked for a 5% service charge for smaller businesses, so it's worth confirming the terms beforehand.

Tipping Culture in Croatia

Tipping in Croatia is customary but not obligatory, and it's appreciated for good service. The standard tip is around **10%** of the total bill in restaurants, cafes, and bars, though if the service is exceptional, you can leave more. For taxis, rounding up the fare to the nearest 10 kuna is common practice.

For other services like hotel staff, porters, or tour guides, a tip of 20-50 kuna ($3-$7 USD) is appropriate, depending on the level of service provided. Don't feel pressured to tip if the service wasn't up to standard, but it's always a nice gesture when the service exceeds your expectations.

Health & Safety: Staying Safe in Zadar

Zadar is a safe city for travelers, and violent crime is rare. However, like any popular tourist destination, there are a few precautions to keep in mind to ensure your safety:

- **Petty Theft**: Pickpocketing can occur, especially in crowded tourist areas like the

Green Market or while using public transport. Keep your belongings close and avoid displaying large amounts of cash or valuables.

- **Health Services**: Croatia has a well-developed healthcare system. For minor issues, pharmacies are easy to find (many are open from 8:00 AM to 8:00 PM). In case of an emergency, dial **112** for ambulances or the police.

- **Sun Protection**: The Adriatic sun can be very strong, especially in summer, so make sure to wear sunscreen, drink plenty of water, and take breaks in the shade.

Wi-Fi & SIM Cards: Staying Connected

Most cafes, restaurants, and hotels in Zadar offer **free Wi-Fi**, though the quality can vary. For reliable internet access, it's a good idea to check with your accommodation about the Wi-Fi speeds or use cafes with good reviews for internet connectivity.

If you need mobile data, buying a local SIM card is a great option. Major Croatian mobile carriers include **T-Mobile**, **A1**, and **Tele2**, and you can buy a prepaid SIM card with data at Zadar's airport, kiosks, or official stores in the city center. Expect to pay around **100-150 HRK** ($15-$25 USD) for a SIM card with 10GB of data, which should be sufficient for basic browsing and navigation.

14 Sustaina

ble & Responsible

Tourism in Zadar

How to Travel Consciously and Respectfully

Zadar, a beautiful city nestled along Croatia's Adriatic coast, is known for its rich history, crystal-clear waters, and stunning landscapes. As tourism in the region continues to grow, the importance of sustainable and responsible travel has never been more crucial. If you're looking to experience Zadar while minimizing your impact on the environment and supporting its local community, this guide is for you. From eco-friendly accommodations to ways you can respect the city's heritage, here's how to travel responsibly in one of Croatia's most charming cities.

Eco-Friendly Accommodations & Tours

When you're planning your stay in Zadar, choosing eco-friendly accommodations is an easy way to reduce your environmental footprint. Many hotels and private rentals are increasingly adopting sustainable practices, from energy-efficient lighting and water-saving measures to waste reduction and local sourcing of food.

1. Falkensteiner Hotel & Spa Iadera

Address: Punta Skala bb, 23231, Zadar
This 5-star luxury hotel is an excellent choice for eco-conscious travelers. Falkensteiner Hotel & Spa Iadera incorporates green technologies, including energy-efficient heating and cooling systems, and the use of sustainable building materials. Additionally, the hotel focuses on supporting local products in its restaurants and encourages guests to minimize waste. The hotel is located near the sea, which allows for easy access to outdoor activities like hiking and cycling, both of which are great alternatives to motorized transport. Prices at Falkensteiner start from **$200 per night** for a standard double room, with wellness packages available for an additional fee.

2. Boutique Hostel Forum

Address: Trg Petra Zoranića 4, 23000 Zadar
For a more budget-conscious yet eco-friendly option, Boutique Hostel Forum is located right in the heart of Zadar's Old Town, within walking distance to major

attractions. This modern hostel embraces sustainability with its use of locally sourced furnishings, a waste recycling program, and the promotion of reusable items such as water bottles. Rates at the hostel range from **$40 to $60 per night**, depending on the season and room type.

3. Eco Tours & Nature Excursions When it comes to tours, opting for eco-friendly excursions is a great way to explore Zadar's surrounding areas without negatively impacting the environment. Many tour operators in Zadar now offer guided hikes, bike tours, and boat excursions that minimize the use of carbon-intensive vehicles. Look for providers that utilize electric boats or smaller, eco-conscious vessels for tours to nearby islands such as the Kornati National Park or the tranquil Dugi Otok.

For example, **Zadar Kayak Tours** offers guided tours through the city's canals and along the coastline. Prices for a half-day tour range from **$40 to $50 per person**, and they use eco-friendly kayaks that allow you to silently glide through Zadar's pristine waters without disturbing the natural environment. Booking a kayak tour not only provides a unique perspective of the city's coastline but also ensures that you're making minimal environmental impact.

4. Sustainable Transport Options
For transportation, try using the city's well-developed public transportation system or rent a bicycle. Zadar has an expanding network of bike paths, making cycling a great way to explore the city and its surroundings. You can rent a bike for as little as **$15 per day**, or join a guided eco-tour, which also includes the bike rental.

If you prefer exploring the coastal areas, consider renting an electric scooter or e-bike, which are increasingly popular for short-distance travel. Several rental shops, such as **e-bike Zadar**, offer daily rentals starting at **$25 for an electric scooter** and **$30 for an e-bike**.

How to Support Local Businesses & Artisans
A great way to practice responsible tourism in Zadar is by supporting local businesses and artisans. This not

only helps sustain the local economy but also ensures that the area's cultural heritage is preserved. Here's how to make the most of your time while supporting Zadar's local scene.

1.   Visit   the   Green   Market
Address: Kalelarga,   23000   Zadar
Zadar's Green Market (Tržnica) is a bustling hub of fresh produce, local specialties, and handmade goods. It's the perfect place to interact with local farmers, artisans, and vendors. Here, you'll find everything from fresh fruits and vegetables to handmade soaps, traditional textiles, and artwork. Buying local produce ensures that you're supporting Zadar's agriculture and minimizing the carbon footprint of food production.

Many of the market's vendors practice sustainable farming methods, and you'll often find organic options available. Prices can range from **$2 for a bunch of locally grown organic vegetables** to **$15 for handmade ceramics** crafted by Zadar's artisans.

2. Support Local Artisans at the Museum of Ancient   Glass
Address: Poljana Zemaljskog odbora 1, 23000 Zadar

The Museum of Ancient Glass in Zadar is an excellent example of how tradition and sustainability can go hand-in-hand. This museum is dedicated to preserving and showcasing the ancient glassmaking techniques that were once prevalent in the region. While visiting, you can support local artisans by purchasing handmade glassware created using traditional methods. Expect to pay around **$20 for a small decorative piece** or **$50 for larger glass sculptures**.

In addition to purchasing glass items, you can also attend workshops to learn the ancient craft and gain a deeper appreciation for the skills that have been passed down through generations.

3. Dine at Sustainable Restaurants
Zadar has a growing number of restaurants that focus on using local, seasonal ingredients while minimizing food waste. **Pet Bunara** and **Foša** (which we've mentioned earlier in the accommodation section) are great examples of eateries that emphasize sustainability. By choosing these restaurants, you'll support local farmers and fishermen and help preserve

the environment by eating foods that are in season and less reliant on long-distance transport.

A meal at **Pet Bunara**, for example, averages around **$25-$50 per person**, depending on the dish and wine selection. The restaurant offers a farm-to-table experience that highlights the region's finest seasonal produce, meats, and fish. They prioritize using organic, locally grown ingredients and work with small, local suppliers.

Respecting Zadar's Cultural Heritage & Environment

Being a responsible tourist also means respecting Zadar's natural and cultural heritage. The city is home to a number of historical landmarks and UNESCO-listed sites, which must be preserved for future generations.

1. Preserve the Old Town

Zadar's Old Town is a UNESCO World Heritage Site and a major attraction for visitors. The cobbled streets, ancient Roman ruins, and medieval churches are all delicate and precious remnants of Zadar's long history. While you're here, it's essential to respect the heritage sites and avoid actions that could cause damage, such as graffiti, littering, or walking on fragile historical monuments. Stick to marked paths, avoid disturbing wildlife, and make sure to dispose of waste properly.

2. Protect Marine Life and the Environment Zadar is surrounded by some of Croatia's most beautiful beaches and crystal-clear waters. When you visit beaches like **Kolovare Beach** or the more remote **Saharun Beach** on Dugi Otok, make sure to respect the environment by avoiding littering and refraining from picking up marine life like shells or coral. If you're going swimming or snorkeling, avoid touching the underwater flora and fauna to prevent harm to the ecosystems.

3. Participate in Local Clean-Up Efforts If you want to go the extra mile, consider joining a local beach clean-up effort during your stay. Organizations like **Zadar Eco-Centre** often host events that encourage tourists and locals alike to work together to clean up the beaches and the surrounding natural areas. These activities provide a meaningful way to give back to the community while helping preserve Zadar's natural beauty.

15 Final

Thoughts &

Itinerary

Suggestions

Zadar is one of Croatia's most charming and underrated destinations, where ancient history, natural beauty, and a laid-back coastal vibe come together in perfect harmony. Whether you're spending just a few days or taking your time to explore, Zadar has something for every kind of traveler. To make sure you experience the best of this coastal gem, I've put together a series of suggested itineraries and tips that will help you make the most of your time here.

3-Day Zadar Itinerary for First-Time Visitors

If you're visiting Zadar for the first time, a three-day itinerary gives you enough time to explore the highlights, from its famous landmarks to its stunning coastline.

Day 1: Explore the Old Town and its Ancient Wonders

Start your day by getting familiar with the heart of Zadar, its Old Town, which is home to some of the city's most iconic attractions. After a leisurely breakfast, head to the **Roman Forum** (open from 8:00 AM - 9:00 PM), located just off the main pedestrian street **Kalelarga**. The forum dates back to the 1st century BC and is a magnificent example of Roman architecture. Spend time wandering through its ruins and imagining what life was like during the Roman Empire. Entrance is free.

Next, walk to the **St. Donatus Church** (open from 9:00 AM - 6:00 PM), one of Zadar's most distinctive landmarks. This pre-Romanesque church dates back to the 9th century and its circular structure makes it one of a kind. Entrance costs around **$5**.

For lunch, head to **Bruschetta** for a delicious mix of Italian and Mediterranean dishes. The casual yet modern atmosphere and stunning views make it the perfect spot for a midday break. A meal here costs approximately **$15-$20** per person.

In the afternoon, don't miss the **Sea Organ** (open from 10:00 AM to sunset) and the **Greeting to the Sun** installation (open 24/7), which are both located along the waterfront. These modern marvels use the power of the waves and the sun to create mesmerizing sounds and light shows, respectively. The best time to visit is during sunset when you can experience both the light show and the sound of the waves.

Day 2: Island Exploration and Local Markets

Start your second day early by taking a ferry or a boat excursion to **Dugi Otok** (open year-round). This island is home to **Saharun Beach**, one of the most beautiful and tranquil beaches in the region, known for its clear turquoise waters and sandy shores. You can rent a kayak or paddleboard for **$20** per hour to explore the nearby coves.

On your return to Zadar, make sure to stop by **Zadar's Green Market** (open daily from 7:00 AM - 3:00 PM), which offers an array of fresh, locally grown produce, cheese, cured meats, and handmade crafts. It's a great place to pick up some souvenirs like handmade jewelry or locally produced honey.

In the evening, head to **Foša** for dinner, a waterfront restaurant with an excellent seafood menu. A meal here will set you back around **$40-$50** per person, but the quality and setting are well worth it.

Day 3: Historical Sites and Relaxation

On your final day, begin with a visit to the **Museum of Ancient Glass** (open from 9:00 AM - 8:00 PM). This hidden gem houses an impressive collection of glass artifacts, showcasing the region's ancient history in glassmaking. The entrance fee is around **$8** per person.

Afterward, head to **St. Anastasia's Cathedral** (open from 9:00 AM - 6:00 PM), where you can climb the bell tower for stunning panoramic views of Zadar. The entrance fee is typically **$4**.

In the afternoon, take some time to relax at **Kolovare Beach** (open daily), Zadar's most popular beach. If you prefer a more secluded experience, you can head to **Punta Bajlo**, a lesser-known gem among locals.

In the evening, enjoy your last dinner at **Pet Bunara**, a restaurant that focuses on farm-to-table dining. The price for a meal here averages around **$30-$45** per person, and you can try local specialties like peka, a traditional slow-cooked dish.

5-Day Itinerary Including Day Trips

If you're lucky enough to have five days in Zadar, you'll have more time to take a couple of day trips and fully immerse yourself in the natural and cultural beauty of the region.

Day 1: Old Town and Sunset Views

Follow the same plan as Day 1 of the 3-day itinerary. Explore the Roman Forum, St. Donatus Church, Sea Organ, and Greeting to the Sun. Then, finish the day with a relaxed evening at one of the best local rooftop bars, **The Garden Lounge**. Sip on a cocktail while enjoying sweeping views of the city and the Adriatic Sea.

Day 2: Krka National Park

Take a day trip to **Krka National Park** (open from 7:00 AM - 8:00 PM), about an hour's drive from Zadar. The park is famous for its stunning waterfalls, including **Skradinski Buk**, which is one of the largest and most impressive waterfall systems in Europe. You can walk along the boardwalks and swim in the crystal-clear pools, though swimming may be restricted in certain areas. Expect to pay an entrance fee of **$10** for adults.

Krka Tours offers guided excursions from Zadar starting around **$50** per person, including transport and a tour guide.

Day 3: The Kornati Islands

The Kornati Islands are a must-see for nature lovers. Book a boat trip through one of the local tour operators, such as **Kornati National Park Tours**, for an unforgettable experience. These excursions typically last 6-8 hours, with the price ranging from **$60 to $100** per person depending on the type of tour. The park is famous for its dramatic cliffs, crystal-clear waters, and uninhabited islands. It's the perfect place for a day of swimming, snorkeling, or simply soaking in the natural beauty.

Day 4: Pag Island and Nin

On Day 4, take a day trip to **Pag Island**, known for its lunar landscapes and famous **Pag cheese**. If you're a cheese lover, be sure to visit a local dairy farm and sample the island's signature cheese. You can also explore the **salt pans of Nin**, located about 30 minutes from Zadar. The small town of Nin is home to Roman ruins and a tranquil beach, perfect for a relaxing day.

Day 5: Rest and Relax
Take your final day to rest and relax. Start with a leisurely breakfast at **Art Kavana**, a café in the heart of the Old Town with great coffee and pastries. Then, head back to **Kolovare Beach** or visit **Punta Bajlo** to enjoy the peaceful surroundings before you head home.

A Week in Zadar: The Ultimate Slow Travel Plan

For those with more time to spend, a week in Zadar offers the perfect opportunity for slow travel—taking in the sights at a more leisurely pace, spending time with locals, and truly soaking in the atmosphere.

Day 1-3: Follow the 3-Day Itinerary
Spend the first three days following the **3-Day Zadar Itinerary** mentioned above. Use these days to dive into the city's history, culture, and beauty.

Day 4: Day Trip to Plitvice Lakes National Park

Take a day trip to **Plitvice Lakes National Park** (open year-round), one of Croatia's most famous natural wonders. The park is home to a series of cascading lakes and waterfalls, surrounded by lush forests. The entrance fee is around **$20** for adults, and it's recommended to arrive early to avoid crowds.

Plitvice Lake Tours offers guided trips to the park starting at **$50 per person**, including transport and entry tickets.

Day 5: Kayaking and Relaxing

On Day 5, rent a kayak or stand-up paddleboard and explore the coastline at your own pace. Whether you decide to go to **Dugi Otok** or just explore around Zadar, kayaking is a peaceful way to discover hidden beaches and coves.

Spend your evening at **The Garden Lounge**, where you can watch the sunset while enjoying some cocktails.

Day 6-7: Explore Zadar's Hidden Gems

Finally, take time to explore some of Zadar's hidden gems. Visit **Zadar's Museum of Ancient Glass**, take a walk through **Queen Jelena Madijevka Park**, or discover the lesser-known beach of **Punta Bajlo**. For the final evening, enjoy dinner at **Pet Bunara**, and treat yourself to the best Dalmatian cuisine.

Hidden Gems & Off-the-Beaten-Path Spots

For those looking to venture off the beaten path, here are a few hidden gems:

1. **Vransko Lake Nature Park** – A peaceful nature reserve just 30 minutes from Zadar, perfect for hiking, birdwatching, and cycling.

2. **Island of Ugljan** – A small, quiet island just across the channel from Zadar, ideal for peaceful walks, bike rides, and a swim in the crystal-clear waters.

3. **The Olive Oil Museum** – Located in the town of **Privlaka**, this small museum offers a deep dive into the history of olive oil production in the region.

16 Resource

s & Useful Contacts for Your Zadar Adventure

W hen traveling to a new city, it's always good to be prepared with essential information in case of emergencies or if you simply need some guidance. Zadar, while a beautiful and welcoming destination, is no different in this regard. To ensure your trip goes smoothly, here's a detailed guide to all the resources you might need during your stay in this charming Croatian city.

Emergency Numbers & Hospitals in Zadar

While Zadar is generally a safe city, it's always wise to know the emergency numbers and where to seek medical attention just in case. Croatia, like most of Europe, has standardized emergency services, making it relatively easy for travelers to get the help they need in any situation.

Emergency Numbers:

1. **Police:** Dial **112** (for general emergencies) or **192** (direct police line).

2. **Fire Department:** Dial **112** or **193** (direct line for fire emergencies).

3. **Ambulance:** Dial **112** or **194** (direct line for medical emergencies).

4. **European Emergency Number:** Dial **112** for any emergency throughout the EU.

It's important to note that **112** is the general emergency number for the EU, which is accessible for free from any mobile phone. When calling this number, make sure to clearly state your emergency and your location.

Hospitals in Zadar:

Zadar is well-equipped with hospitals that can provide medical assistance in case of emergencies. Here are the main hospitals and medical facilities in the city:

1. **General Hospital Zadar (Opća bolnica Zadar)**

   o **Address:** Ul. dr. Franje Tuđmana 10, 23000 Zadar, Croatia

   o **Contact:** +385 23 600 800

   o **Open:** 24 hours

- o **Website:** www.ob-zadar.hr

This is the largest hospital in Zadar, providing emergency services, general medical care, and specialized departments. The hospital is easily accessible from the city center, and many services are available round-the-clock.

2. **Private Clinics and Urgent Care:**

   - o **Poliklinika Sunce (Private Polyclinic)**

     - **Address:** Ul. Šime Ljubića 6, 23000 Zadar, Croatia

     - **Contact:** +385 23 309 669

     - **Website:** www.poliklinika-sunce.hr

If you need non-emergency medical services, private clinics such as **Poliklinika Sunce** provide faster access to general practitioners, dentists, and specialists. These clinics can be more expensive, with consultations typically costing between **$30** and **$70**, depending on the type of visit.

Tourist Information Centers

For visitors looking for advice, maps, brochures, and tips on things to do, Zadar's Tourist Information Centers are the perfect places to start your adventure. Here, you can find the latest updates on events, opening hours, and anything you might need during your stay.

Tourist Information Center – Zadar Old Town

- **Address:** Trg pet bunara 1, 23000 Zadar, Croatia

- **Opening Hours:** Monday to Friday: 8:00 AM – 7:00 PM, Saturday: 8:00 AM – 2:00 PM, Sunday: Closed

- **Contact:** +385 23 302 480

- **Website:** www.zadar.travel

This centrally located Tourist Information Center is an excellent resource to learn about Zadar's historical sites, cultural events, and unique tours available. They provide city maps, information on public transport, and can even help with booking excursions like boat trips to the Kornati Islands or guided walking tours.

Tourist Information Center – Zadar Bus Station

- **Address:** Zadar Bus Terminal, 23000 Zadar, Croatia

- **Opening Hours:** Monday to Sunday: 7:00 AM – 9:00 PM

- **Contact:** +385 23 312 522

- **Website:** www.ak-zadar.hr

Located at the Zadar Bus Station, this Tourist Information Center caters to travelers arriving by bus and offers helpful tips for those exploring the surrounding areas, such as trips to nearby national parks or the islands. It's also a good spot for purchasing bus tickets and learning about local transportation.

Embassies & Consulates in Zadar

While Zadar is a peaceful city, it's still important to know where your embassy or consulate is located in case you lose your passport, need consular assistance, or require emergency services. Croatia has embassies and consulates in major cities, but the nearest embassy for Zadar residents would be in **Zagreb**, the capital.

Embassy of the United States (Zagreb)

- **Address:** Ulica Thomas Jeffersona 2, 10010 Zagreb, Croatia

- **Contact:** +385 1 661 2200

- **Website:** hr.usembassy.gov

This embassy is your primary resource for any U.S. citizen-related services, from emergency passports to consular assistance. In case of an emergency, it's best to contact them directly and arrange a visit.

British Embassy (Zagreb)

- **Address:** Trg J. F. Kennedy 1, 10000 Zagreb, Croatia

- **Contact:** +385 1 6009 500

- **Website:** www.gov.uk/world/countries/croatia

The British Embassy in Zagreb offers consular services and can assist with emergency situations, passport issues, and other travel-related concerns.

Other Consulates in Zadar:
If you are a citizen of a country other than the U.S. or the U.K., Zadar does not have any foreign consulates. However, embassies in Zagreb or consular services available in Split can typically assist in emergencies.

Local Blogs & Websites for Up-to-Date Information

To stay informed about what's happening in Zadar, local blogs and websites are a great resource. They offer up-to-date event listings, local news, restaurant recommendations, and insider tips for the best experiences.

1. **Zadar Travel Blog**

    o **Website:** www.zadar.travel

    o **Description:** The official travel website of Zadar, this blog provides comprehensive guides, event calendars, and a deep dive into the best things to do in Zadar. It's an excellent resource for tourists looking for local insight, whether it's about historic landmarks or where to grab a delicious meal.

2. **Zadar News**

   o **Website:** www.zadarnews.hr

   o **Description:** For the latest news and happenings in Zadar, **Zadar News** is an invaluable resource. It features local news updates, weather forecasts, and articles about cultural events in the city. Whether you're curious about a public festival or wondering when the next big event is, Zadar News has you covered.

3. **The Dubrovnik Times**

   o **Website:** www.dubrovniktimes.com

   o **Description:** Although based in Dubrovnik, **The Dubrovnik Times** provides updates and news about the entire Dalmatian region, including Zadar. It's a great resource for information about regional travel, upcoming events, and things to do in nearby areas like Split and Sibenik.

Conclusion

Your Ultimate Guide to Zadar – A City Like No Other

Zadar is an extraordinary destination, blending natural beauty, rich history, and modern attractions into one seamless experience. From ancient Roman ruins to the contemporary marvels of the Sea Organ and Greeting to the Sun, the city offers something for every type of traveler. Whether you are seeking a relaxing beach vacation, a cultural journey, or thrilling outdoor adventures, Zadar will not disappoint.

Embrace the Rich History and Culture of Zadar

Zadar's historical landmarks are undeniably some of its most prominent features. From the **Roman Forum** to **St. Donatus Church**, the city is a living museum of its past. Take the time to explore the **Zadar City**

Walls and Gates, which served as defense mechanisms for centuries, and enjoy the walk around the walls, which offer spectacular views of the surrounding sea and islands. These landmarks are not just stones and structures—they are windows into the past that tell stories of Roman emperors, Venetian rule, and Croatian resilience.

For a truly immersive experience, visit the **Museum of Ancient Glass**, where you can admire unique glass artifacts from the Roman Empire or walk through the historical streets of the old town. These are the places where you will connect with Zadar's unique narrative.

Nature at Its Finest

Zadar is blessed with some of the most awe-inspiring natural wonders. From the sparkling waters of the **Kornati Islands** to the pristine landscapes of **Plitvice Lakes National Park** and **Krka National Park**, you can lose yourself in the beauty of the Croatian outdoors. Day trips to these locations are an absolute must if you're in Zadar for more than just a couple of days. Even if you only have one day, a boat ride through the Kornati archipelago will leave you with unforgettable memories of turquoise waters, rocky shores, and the refreshing sea breeze.

If you prefer exploring on foot, there are stunning **hiking and cycling routes near Zadar** that will take you through nature reserves, hills, and along the coast, offering magnificent views and moments of solitude. For adrenaline seekers, don't miss **paragliding** or **skydiving over the Adriatic**, where the thrill of soaring above the islands will leave you breathless.

The Delicious Flavors of Zadar

One of the greatest pleasures of visiting Zadar is undoubtedly the food. The city's cuisine reflects the flavors of Dalmatia, where fresh ingredients and simple preparation shine through. Try the **Peka**, a traditional Dalmatian dish of slow-cooked meat or seafood. Head to **Konoba Skoblar** for an authentic meal where you can savor the taste of Croatian tradition. If seafood is your passion, you'll find plenty of fresh options, such as octopus salad and grilled fish, on menus across town.

Pag cheese and **Dalmatian wines** are another great treat. These local specialties are available in abundance at various markets and eateries. Be sure to visit **Konzum Market** or **Pazar Market** for a range of products, including local cheese, cured meats, and fresh fruits and vegetables. The local **Maraschino liqueur**, crafted from cherries, is the perfect Croatian souvenir to bring home or enjoy with friends.

Zadar's Vibrant Festivals & Events

Zadar isn't just a city to visit; it's a city to experience. Its annual festivals and events are a big part of the city's charm. The **Zadar Sunset Festival** offers music, DJs, and beach vibes, while the **Full Moon Festival** takes place on the beach with a magical night market by the sea. These events are an ideal way to experience Zadar's lively spirit and meet fellow travelers.

If you're in Zadar during the winter months, the **Advent in Zadar** Christmas celebration transforms the city into a festive wonderland with twinkling lights, food stalls, and holiday cheer. These festivals allow you to immerse yourself in the local culture, music, and food while enjoying the company of both locals and visitors.

Relaxation and Adventure at Zadar's Beaches

Zadar's beaches are more than just places to swim—they offer different experiences depending on what kind of traveler you are. **Kolovare Beach** is a popular choice, perfect for those who want to swim and enjoy a classic beach day. If you prefer quieter spots, head to **Punta Bajlo**, a hidden gem favored by locals. **Saharun Beach**, located on Dugi Otok, is a true slice of paradise, accessible by ferry for a day trip. And for families or water sports enthusiasts, **Borik Beach** is perfect, offering water activities and a family-friendly atmosphere.

These beaches will provide you with everything from peace and relaxation to adventure and exploration. It's all about knowing which one fits your style, whether it's swimming in clear waters, soaking up the sun, or trying your hand at water sports.

Making the Most of Your Time in Zadar

To truly make the most of your visit, plan your itinerary in advance. Zadar offers a lot, but it's essential to give yourself time to enjoy each experience. If you're a first-time visitor, consider a 3-day itinerary that covers the highlights, such as the **Sea Organ**, **Greeting to the Sun**, and some beach time, as well as a day trip to one of the national parks. If you have more time, a 5-day itinerary allows for a deeper exploration of nearby islands or a visit to **Nin**, the oldest royal town in Croatia.

For the ultimate slow travel experience, spend a week in Zadar. Take it slow. Wander through the streets, sip coffee at one of the charming cafés, and let Zadar's beauty and history unfold at your own pace.

Essential Travel Tips & Practical Info

Traveling to Zadar is an easy and convenient experience, thanks to its well-connected airport, local transportation, and helpful tourist information centers. In terms of budgeting, Croatia remains one of the more affordable European destinations, with meals at mid-range restaurants costing around **$20-$30** per person, and public transport easily accessible for less than **$3** per ride.

When visiting Zadar, try to avoid peak summer months (July and August) as the city can get crowded. Spring and fall offer pleasant weather, fewer tourists, and the best opportunity to enjoy the local sights and culture without the rush.

Printed in Great Britain
by Amazon

59899234R00117